Micro Meditation

Micro Meditation

*Moments of calm for a happier,
healthier life*

Nicci Roscoe

CICO BOOKS
LONDON NEW YORK

Published in 2025 by CICO Books
An imprint of Ryland Peters & Small Ltd
20–21 Jockey's Fields
London WC1R 4BW
and
1452 Davis Bugg Road
Warrenton, NC 27589

www.rylandpeters.com

10 9 8 7 6 5 4 3 2 1

Text © Nicci Roscoe 2025
Design and illustration © CICO Books 2025

A CIP catalog record for this book is
available from the Library of Congress
and the British Library.

ISBN: 978-1-80065-409-9

Printed in China

Illustrator: Camila Gray
For additional picture credits, see page 143

Project editor: Kristy Richardson
Senior designer: Emily Breen
Art director: Sally Powell
Creative director: Leslie Harrington
Production manager: Gordana Simakovic
Head of production: Patricia Harrington
Publishing manager: Carmel Edmonds

Note: If you or a family member, friend,
or colleague have any mental health issues
that you notice are getting worse, or sleep
deprivation issues that continue, please contact
your doctor or health professional for advice.
Please note that while the descriptions of the
properties of some crystals refer to healing
qualities, they are not intended to replace
diagnosis of illness or ailments, or healing
or medicine. Always consult your doctor or
other health professional in the case of illness.

To my amazing father, Michael Roscoe.

This book is dedicated to my father, Michael Roscoe, who
took such an interest in everyone he met, always making
them feel special. He loved to read and learn, and his
wonderful qualities made him who he was. He was always
open to me helping him with ways to feel better mentally
and physically through meditation and positive thinking and
also to experiencing holistic healing, including Reiki and
crystals. There were many times of laughter along the
way! He wanted to experience my micro meditations,
and I was always giving him new ones, which gave him
moments of calm and peace along with times of joy and
laughter. I'll always have him with me and hear his wise
words of wisdom and his fun sense of humor.

Wherever you are in the world, if you're suffering
challenges, or know someone who is going through their
own emotional turmoil, these micro meditations will help
you in the moment. This book will bring you calm, peace,
and comfort throughout your day, and most of all bring
you back into the present to be you again.

I send you much love, strength, and compassion from my
heart to yours. You can do this! You can get through your
challenges and open your mind, just like my father did, to
explore new ways to change your mindset and feel better.
I dedicate this book to you, too.

Big hugs,

Contents

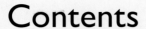

Introduction

The wonderful experience of becoming a mum and a grandmother is a blessing and has given me so much. In the working world, too, from being Head of Aerobics for a group of health and fitness clubs, to a career in fashion and beauty magazines and being a presenter on national television and radio, I have noticed so much about life in the outside world and what it can throw at you. Relationships with loved ones—and everyone you meet while walking the road of life—can test you to your limits and I know how it feels to be worried or constantly on the go. Sometimes you just need to stop, scream, sleep, or simply have some fun time for yourself!

When I discovered I had a brain tumor in 2001 (see page 43), I was determined to draw on everything positive I had learned to help myself and others. I wanted to feel better—and I'd love to help you feel better too—with techniques that make a positive difference, whatever you are going through. Traditional meditation gives me peace, clarity, and so much more. I wanted something similar, without having to plan specific times to do it. And so, this book was born. Micro meditations will give you time-out mentally from whatever is happening, when you need it. They are so effective, and I love how they do what you need them to, very quickly! I want to share them with you because they are all amazing distractions that can help you in your daily life.

From me to you, this book comes from all the experiences I have had so far, with love, care, hope, and excitement. I hope you will utilize these micro meditations in every aspect of your life, whenever you need to feel better in an instant.

> "One moment can change a day, one day can change a life, and one life can change the world."
>
> BUDDHA

WHAT ARE MICRO MEDITATIONS?

Micro meditations are short, quick, and effective distractions that will help you refocus your mindset in less than two minutes throughout your day. These mini "moments of change" will enable you to manage feelings of frustration, anxiety, or overwhelm. They will allow you to take control of your emotions and feel calmer, more peaceful, and happier from within.

Butterflies are a beautiful representation of change and hope. The transformation you go through as you cope with challenging times, by focusing on your micro meditation several times during the day, is a process just like the birth of a butterfly. From fragile and vulnerable like a tiny egg to taking your first steps like the tiny caterpillar that is discovering the freedom to explore nature, you, too, will learn to take slow, deep breaths to help you feel calm and become more aware of how to manage your emotions, whatever is going on around you. As you focus on your micro meditations throughout your day, an amazing transformation takes place—just as the caterpillar metamorphoses into a chrysalis, so these amazing tools will help you change in the moment. When you are ready, you will emerge and fly free like a butterfly, feeling stronger, more in control, happier, and confident to move forward with your life.

THE BENEFITS OF MICRO MEDITATION

A regular meditation practice morning and evening is very beneficial. But not everyone has the time or the mental capacity to meditate for long periods each day. Unlike longer, traditional meditations, micro meditations break your cycle of stress in a moment, without having to spend up to an hour every time you meditate. They give you an immediate focus, taking your attention away from what is frustrating or upsetting you, and helping you feel so much better in less than two minutes—some only take a few magical seconds.

Micro meditations are quick, effective, and powerful. They will help you to manage everyday stresses and lift your mood in moments, whether you are at home with the kids, commuting every day, working in the office, going through a relationship breakup, multitasking, or simply doing everyday things that bring out the frustration in you. They can be done anytime or anywhere throughout the day, without anyone else noticing! In today's modern world, we live life at a very fast pace, but regular practice can help you make the changes you need to manage your daily lifestyle and routine.

By bringing your attention into the present moment with these positive distractions, micro meditation sends a message to your brain to reset and feel so much better.

Overwhelm, upset, anger, worry, and more can be managed with micro meditation. Every time you feel overwhelmed or stressed, STOP! Take a moment to do a micro meditation and in less than two minutes you will feel calmer and more in control. With your mind focused, you will feel calmer and have more clarity when managing your

emotions. The more you manage your mood, the more you can take care of your own health and well-being and improve your mental fitness.

If you're feeling overwhelmed, stressed, anxious, or fatigued, and don't feel you have the motivation to do anything, micro meditation will help you to de-stress and get back on track. It takes just a moment for micro meditations to refresh, revitalize, and give you a total boost of energy. Giving yourself this brief moment of peace and quiet at different times throughout the day can do wonders to refresh your mindset and lift your mood.

If you have experienced trauma in your life that has prevented you from moving forward, these micro meditations will help distract you in the moment. However, the stress of a traumatic memory or a recent trauma you have gone through may need longer, traditional meditations, or even specific therapy, to help you find a way to acknowledge and accept what has happened and to learn different coping skills and cognitive exercises to help you. You may never forget what happened, but it can become a distant memory. Introducing micro meditations into your life can bring you back into the present, give you the peace and calm you may need in the moment, and give you the opportunity to live your life in a way you hadn't dreamed would be possible.

HOW TO USE THIS BOOK

Looking through this book is like walking into a candy store and finding the perfect sweet treat, or like going shopping for a special occasion and finding just the right outfit to help you feel amazing. In the following chapters, I want to give you something you can dip into at any time, to find a micro meditation that is exactly right for you in that moment.

At times you may feel frustrated because your children aren't listening to you. Or perhaps you are feeling overwhelmed because your boss or work colleague is putting you in a time-pressured situation, or maybe you feel hurt because you've experienced a relationship breakup. These are just are some of the situations you may find yourself in that micro meditations can help you manage. There are many different micro meditations to help you, from a moment of indulgence with a tub of ice cream to boosting energy with a two-minute power walk—there are so many ways you can switch challenging emotions to positive distractions! Each meditation will give you the headspace you need to feel calm and take control of your feelings in the moment, so you can manage whatever is causing upset or turmoil in your life. Have fun exploring the different micro meditations, including those with crystals (see pages 116–135), which can bring a whole new dimension to various situations. Throughout the book there are also case studies of clients I have worked with, which give examples of how the meditations might relate to different situations. Keep your micro meditation book nearby as you learn to mix and match your meditations with your mood and enhance your well-being for a healthier and happier lifestyle.

"Mindfulness helps you go home to the present. And every time you go there and recognize a condition of happiness that you have, happiness comes."

THICH NHAT HANH

Chapter 1

Managing Stress and Challenging Emotions

Breaking Your Cycle of Stress

When you start to worry about a situation and everything feels too much, it's time to take action. Focus on taking care of yourself before your physical and mental symptoms begin to spiral. Everyday situations can manifest into a huge burden, and burnout and physical and mental exhaustion can take over, preventing you from managing.

When you worry, it may be because you are anticipating what could happen without knowing whether it ever will or not. You may be afraid of "what if" scenarios:

- "What if I lose my job?"

- "What if I can't pay next month's bills?"

- "What if my friend doesn't speak to me again?"

- "What if I become unwell?"

- "Why hasn't my recent hot date called or messaged me?"

STOP thinking these thoughts right now and START introducing micro meditations. Practicing them throughout your day will bring you back to the present moment. This will enable you to catch these thoughts and manage them before they affect your mental health and well-being.

When you constantly focus on the negative, your unconscious mind absorbs it—focusing on the same pessimistic thoughts and sending negative messages to your brain. The more you worry, the more this can escalate into anxiety, and in turn, this becomes a stressful and emotional turmoil that you get stuck in, affecting your concentration, memory, sleep patterns, confidence, relationships, and so much more. By not managing negativity before it gets too much, you may be compromising your own health and well-being.

Your mind is one of the most powerful assets you have! It controls how you feel, what you say, what you do, and decisions you make. By focusing on positive outcomes, you can take away the pressure of your negative thoughts and give yourself breathing space. There are many situations that can trigger your emotional and physical feelings, such as finances, relationships, breakups, career, grief, moving home and health. By changing your outlook, and focusing on what you CAN do, you can make a positive difference.

Bringing yourself back into the present moment can change your outlook on any situation by helping you take control of your negative thoughts and focus on the now.

Anxiety Takeover

When anxiety takes over and panic sets in, it can feel as if your mind is going into overdrive. Everyone deals with challenging situations in a different way; maybe you suffer from headaches, sweats, or sleepless nights. These feelings can be triggered by lots of different situations, such as:

- Anxiety about a job interview.

- Nerves about an exam.

- Fear of flying.

- Trepidation of walking into a roomful of people on your own.

Feeling anxious can bring on all kinds of emotions that can affect you day and night, but finding the right tools and micro meditations can help you to control what you are feeling. Taking a few deep breaths (see opposite) can calm you down in any situation, and is the perfect pattern interrupter to stop your emotions spiraling in the moment. There are other great cognitive tools to help you take control in the moment, including the self-talk micro meditation (see page 59), anchoring (see page 40), and visualization (see pages 36–37).

REAL LIFE STORY
TAKING CONTROL OF ANXIETY

Mike worked for a fashion company in New York and was petrified of flying. He was expected to plan a fashion event in Los Angeles, and he was so anxious about going that he couldn't concentrate on his job, wasn't sleeping, and kept getting awful headaches.

Mike booked a session with me to help manage his anxiety. We worked on different micro meditations, which included imagining he was relaxing in his favorite chair at home watching a movie with a drink he loved, instead of sitting on the plane. He focused on Positive Affirmations (see pages 64–65), such as "I can do this," and held green calcite (see page 121) to calm him. These short and effective meditations helped Mike feel more in control of his anxiety about flying. The more he focused on being excited about going to LA and do the fashion show, the more Mike started to relax and enjoy what he was doing.

micro meditation
TAKE A DEEP BREATH

A simple, deep breath can take you from panic to peaceful in an instant. The deep breaths you take send a message to your brain and nervous system, relaxing your mind and body and helping you to release the anxiety and stress you are feeling. In moments of panic, when you feel your heart racing and your pulse beating fast, this quick and effective micro meditation will enable you to feel so much more in control and peaceful.

1   The moment you feel panic, for example if your palms feel sweaty or your pulse is racing, take a slow, deep breath in through your nose and slowly breathe out through your mouth.

2   Notice how your shoulders rise up toward your ears as you breath in and drop down again as you breath out.

3   Repeat twice more and feel the difference in moments. Feel the panic fade away as a calm, peaceful feeling washes over you.

micro meditation
FOCUS WHERE YOU FEEL

This is a quick and effective breathing micro meditation
to help you cope with stress and anxiety.

1 Place one hand on your heart and one hand on your tummy.

2 Take a slow breath in through your nose and slowly release
out through your mouth.

3 As you breathe, feel the movement of your tummy going in and out. Focusing on this
movement will distract you from any anxious thoughts you are having in the moment.

micro meditation
RELEASE YOUR ANXIETY

This micro meditation is a technique you can practice discreetly anytime and anywhere,
to calm you in an instant.

1 Take a slow breath in through your nose and slowly release
out through your mouth.

2 Tap gently and slowly over your heart three times
with the palm of your hand.

3 As you do the last tap, hold your hand
over your chest, take a deep breath in,
and as you release say "I'm okay" or
"It's okay," depending on the situation.

4 Repeat three times.

5 Take a slow, deep breath in through
your nose and slowly release out
through your mouth. Feel the change
in you in this short time.

REAL LIFE STORY
MAGGIE'S WORRIES AND WOES

Maggie worried about everything! If she'd forgotten to shut the cap on her toothpaste, she would worry it would go moldy. If her bank account was three dollars overdrawn, she would worry her rent wouldn't get paid (even though she had a 300-dollar overdraft on her account and her paycheck was going in that day). Maggie focused on worrying about things that were not going to happen. She predicted the worst outcomes for every situation.

During her first session with me, I asked her to practice different micro meditations every time she had a worry wobble (see page 20). The Give Yourself Headspace micro meditation (see page 63) and counting backward from ten (see page 47) interrupted her worry pattern. She also loved the Squish, Squeeze, Roll, and Press micro meditation (see page 21) and carried a small pot of play dough in her purse for emergencies, as well as keeping it by her bed in case she had a worry wobble at night. Maggie also started changing her negative thought patterns by focusing on positive outcomes (see pages 58–61).

Now when Maggie goes out, if she leaves the cap off the toothpaste she knows she can just squeeze the top bit out, throw it away, and have the fresh toothpaste at the top. She has stopped worrying. The moment her mind starts to wander, she tells herself STOP! And enjoys all her micro-meditation, worry-wobble, pattern-interrupters!

WORRY WOBBLES

Are you a worry wobbler? Do you constantly worry about the smallest of things, such as:

- Did you forget to have your green juice this morning?

- Are there enough cookies in the cookie jar?

- Are you running out of your breakfast cereal?

- Have you lost one of your earrings?

- Where did you put your favorite shirt?

- Are you worried about how you look?

A worry wobbler is exactly as it sounds—someone who has wobbles when they worry! Maybe your wobbles include panicking, shouting, palpitations, finding it difficult to catch your breath, or breaking out into a sweat. By distracting yourself with a micro meditation every time you have a worry wobble, you can stop the thoughts in moments, bring yourself back into the present, and in time begin to change your mindset.

If you're a worry wobbler, keep practicing micro meditations, such as the Squish, Squeeze, Roll, and Press micro meditation (see opposite), throughout your day. Other wonderful micro meditations in the moment include Scream and Release (see page 23), Laughter Moments to De-stress (see page 28), and Your Musical Distraction (see page 100). Life will never be the same again; the wobbles will go in an instant every time and you will notice how much you love this new, worry-free feeling!

WORRY IS TAKING OVER

STOP!
AND DO A MICRO MEDITATION

RETURN TO PRESENT MOMENT

WORRY IS UNDER CONTROL

micro meditation
SQUISH, SQUEEZE, ROLL, AND PRESS

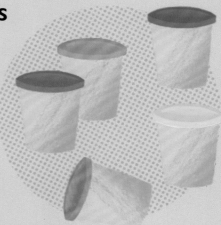

I love doing this micro meditation in my Manage Your Stress workshop—it's perfect for worry wobblers! Everyone's mood immediately changes to playful and happy as they become totally entranced! It's fun and great to do with the kids too.

1 Invest in a tiny pot of playdough or slime to keep with you in your bag, jacket or coat pocket, by the side of your computer, or nightstand. Choose a fun, bright color you love!

2 If you're feeling anxious or having a worry wobble, press your fingers into the playdough or slime, squish it, squeeze it, or roll it!

3 Notice how your focus changes as you feel the cool and squidgy texture.

4 Do this for up to two minutes, as many times throughout your day as needed.

Overwhelm Overload

If you never press the pause button and keep going, there comes a time when overwhelm and exhaustion take over and your energy levels feel depleted as you begin to feel totally run down. It can seem as if your chores are never done, with never-ending food shopping, cleaning, cooking, laundry, and more. Perhaps the following also sounds familiar:

- Are you always rushing in the mornings to get the children to school, making sure they're washed and dressed, sorting out their bag lunch, and getting yourself ready too?

- Are you often late for meetings because there are always non-stop phone calls and messages, or there's more and more work piling up on your desk?

- Do you even have a social life, or has it faded into oblivion because you're staying late at work every night?

- Do you spend your weekends trying to catch up on chores and family obligations?

- Are you suffering from headaches, backache, or lack of sleep?

- When was the last time you took a break from work? Or had a full day off without checking your phone? When did you last stop for some "me time" during your baby's nap instead of catching up on housework?

Eventually, the pressure will affect you physically and mentally if you don't slow down and take time to stop and breathe throughout your busy day. Taking time to find balance during the day can make a huge difference to how you feel. Micro meditation can help you to manage your health and well-being needs and avoid overwhelm overload. Try the micro meditation below, Splash Away Your Overwhelm (see page 29), or Count and Breathe in Stressful Moments (see page 49) to help with different situations when overwhelm takes over.

micro meditation
SCREAM AND RELEASE!

Whenever I think of this micro meditation, it makes me smile because it is a fabulous release that is especially wonderful if it's all too much at home and the kids are driving you crazy, or everyone is asking you a million questions! It's also a great one if you're feeling frustrated at work or anywhere else. You'll need a pillow or cushion.

1 When you feel that it's all getting too much, run into your bedroom or the bathroom with your pillow or cushion.

2 Sit on the toilet seat or your bed and let out a big scream into your cushion or pillow.

3 And BREATHE! It's a fabulous release.

LACKING IN SLEEP AND EXHAUSTED!

It's easy to become overwhelmed if sleep deprivation is preventing you from coping with your daily routine at work or home. Concentrating in meetings at work or online can become a huge challenge and a lack of sleep can also be detrimental to your health, leaving you feeling stressed and irritable, among other unpleasant symptoms.

Everyone requires different amounts of sleep, and it depends on what your body needs to give you the energy you require. Eating well and making sure you're hydrated by drinking plenty of water is a key factor in helping you manage your day, while tips to ensure a good night's sleep include:

- Avoiding stimulants like coffee or sugar late at night.

- Planning to have a good 6–8 hours' sleep a night.

- Getting into the habit of a relaxing bedtime routine.

- Avoiding staying up late on your computer or scrolling through your cell phone.

- Catching up on missed hours of sleep with a power nap. If you're out partying all night, you need to sleep it off! Or if you're up all night with a new baby or toddler, it's important to sleep as much as possible when your little one does.

Introduce short and effective micro meditations into your daily routine. Crystals can give you what need to help you relax. Try the malachite meditation or the garnet power nap (see page 117), which can help give you an energy reset. Check out Embracing Nature's Distractions (see pages 74–87) or try A Cup of Winter Comfort micro meditation (see page 85) every night if it helps you—it's not just restricted to winter! It's very relaxing before bedtime and focuses your mind on the present moment.

micro meditation
OUT OF YOUR HEAD AND ONTO PAPER!

Getting a good night's rest can be challenging if you are feeling overwhelmed, especially if your head is spinning with thoughts going round and round when you go to bed. Clear your mind in less than two minutes with this micro meditation. It's a quick mindset release and gives you space to breathe and sleep with a clear mind, too!

1 Always keep a pen and paper—or even a sleep journal, if you prefer—by your bed. It is important to avoid using your phone before going to bed, which can be overstimulating when you are preparing to snooze.

2 After completing your evening routine of brushing your teeth and getting into bed, jot down any thoughts and feelings about the day you've had or any anxieties and uncertainties you may have about the following day.

3 If you wake up during the night with things on your mind, reach for your paper and pen and write them down before going back to sleep.

4 In the morning, notice how much more rested you feel. Writing your thoughts down can clear your head and help you prepare for the next day. It's a huge relief to get everything out of your head onto the paper.

You can also try this micro meditation during your day if everything is becoming overwhelming. Carry your pen and paper in your bag, or keep them on your desk at work, so you can reach for them quickly.

micro meditation
BOXING YOUR THOUGHTS

If you have family, relationship, financial, or work problems, or any other issues that are constantly on your mind all at once, it can be overwhelming. This micro meditation is a useful tool for handling the things you are concerned, frustrated, or anxious about, and will give you a break from thinking about them all the time.

1 Visualize several boxes going around inside your head.

2 Imagine putting each of your worries into a separate box and closing the lid. You may even want to visualize locking the boxes with a key! This will give you time and space to think.

3 When you are ready to think about your issue, get into a comfortable space where you won't be disturbed. Open one box at a time and focus on this only.

4 Keep practicing! In time, you will see each issue more clearly and give yourself the space you need to put your thoughts into action, without having lots of chatterboxes going on in your head at the same time.

BREAK THE TENSION

There are lots of situations that can make you feel overwhelmed; when you just want some peace and quiet and you feel as if you're about to boil over! Lots of situations can make us feel tension, which then contributes to overwhelm:

• Your kids are on vacation from school and driving you crazy!

• An annoying colleague is not doing what they should and is blaming you in front of your boss.

• A friend has let you down and you haven't spoken to them for a few days.

• You're stuck in the office and late for a date.

• You're at home with a pile of washing and screaming kids who want their dinner.

When life is getting you down, there's no time to have even ten minutes to yourself, and you are literally bubbling over, try these two micro meditations (below and opposite) to break the tension.

micro meditation
LAUGHTER MOMENTS TO DE-STRESS

Think of a funny moment! Find a photo that makes you laugh and use it as the screen saver on your phone. Put a picture up on your fridge door or by your bed. Looking at the more humorous side of life will lighten your mood, and as you continue to remind yourself, it will give you a different perspective on everything in moments.

It may sound like an impossible task when you're in this headspace, but the greatest gift you can give yourself to enhance your mood is to tap into a funny moment and just laugh! Laughter lightens your mood by releasing endorphins (your body's natural feel-good chemicals—the same ones you have when you exercise). It takes you into a completely different place and space in your head while releasing physical tension, as your whole body embraces it, and brings you into the present moment, which helps you refocus and calm your feelings of worry, frustration, and tension.

Funny memories can snap us out of challenging thoughts or situations and give us back a feeling of control. Maybe you were with your friends at a comedy evening, and you laughed so much you had bellyache at the end of it and your voice was hoarse for days! Or maybe you experienced a funny situation, and you and your friend have been laughing about it ever since.

Or perhaps on occasion you feel embarrassed—the best medicine for that is laughing at yourself! Start taking yourself less seriously and look at the funny side of how you've been reacting to a situation. Your friends, partner, or colleagues will probably laugh too, as you are taking everything less seriously. You'll notice in a moment how the atmosphere will change from tense to fun!

micro meditation
SPLASH AWAY YOUR OVERWHELM

An instant and very effective micro meditation is to splash cold water over your face. It will help you to get perspective in an instant as your nervous system is literally shocked, returning you back into the moment where you can reassess your situation, realize that it's not as bad as you thought, and you can handle it! A great alternative is to use a water spray for a quick spritz.

REAL LIFE STORY
A FUNNY MOMENT REMEMBERED

Sally invited her friend Arianne over for the evening. It was a hot, summer's night and all the windows and doors were open to the backyard. Suddenly, what looked like a bat flew into the room! They both screamed and ran out into the hall, laughing so much they could barely speak!

Arianne decided to brave it and go back into the room to see where this bat was. She put a hat on, as she was concerned it would get tangled in her hair. Meanwhile, Sally and her dog Max ran into the kitchen to keep them both safe. Arianne called her to come and help but Sally was too petrified to come out and said she was looking after Max. About ten minutes later, Arianne found Sally and Max huddled up together in the kitchen.

It was a tiny bird, not a bat, which then flew out of the living room and up the stairs! They called the local animal service who finally freed the poor little bird. Arianne and Sally had really thought it was a bat and Sally was still clinging on to Max feeling totally traumatized by the experience! They continue to laugh about it to this day. Arianne is always reminding Sally how she hid in the kitchen with Max, petrified of this tiny bird!

Laughter is absolutely the best medicine! It changes your mood in an instant and gives you a new perspective on a situation. If you're feeling low and need a boost, remember a time that made you laugh.

Frustrating Situations

It can be so frustrating when things don't go your way! You can feel various emotions such as irritation, anger, or tearfulness. There are so many different situations that can bring out the frustration in you:

- You're stuck in traffic and your frustration is verging on road rage as most of the other cars are hooting and shouting at each other and not going anywhere.

- Sitting in the doctor's or dentist's surgery and feeling frustrated because your appointment is over an hour late. Sometimes waiting for your appointment can be more stressful than having it!

- Maybe your new hot date hasn't turned up.

- Your assistant keeps forgetting to do what you ask them and is very slow!

Whatever the situation, unless you take control of your emotions, your pulse can start racing, your heart can start beating faster, and your mood can escalate into anger and more if you don't take control. Frustration can pass quickly if you slow down and take a

REAL LIFE STORY
BREATHE, CALM DOWN, AND RATIONALIZE

My friend Susie phoned to say her washing machine was broken. She was going away in two days and was so frustrated as she had so much laundry to do! She was feeling very upset and talking so fast I couldn't even understand her! The first thing I said was to breathe and slow down, which is the perfect, in-the-moment micro meditation. Once she took a few slow, deep breaths, she started to calm down and could think more rationally. I live too far away for her to bring her washing to me, but her next-door neighbor was lovely, and she asked her if she could borrow her machine. Susie was so relieved when she said yes!

deep breath. Slow, deep breaths are wonderful for relaxing you in the moment and will help you take control of your emotions, giving you time to see if you can find a solution.

There are many different instant micro meditations that will help you manage your frustration as you feel it building up inside you. The secret is to notice when it starts to happen and do something about it in the moment.

The Take a Deep Breath micro meditation (see page 17) will help you, as well as other micro meditations, including Anchor Away Your Frustrations (see page 40) and The Two-Minute Power Walk (see page 34). Walking is also one of the best exercises you can do, not just for your body, but to help clear your mind and give you time to breathe, find clarity, and discover answers to questions for which you've been struggling to find solutions.

micro meditation
THE TWO-MINUTE POWER WALK

The two-minute power walk is a micro meditation that will give you the breathing space to manage frustration in a short time. Try it at different times during your day, in a place outside that you can walk for two minutes, especially if you're at work and need a boost of energy or creativity too. It is also a wonderful exercise that doesn't put as much pressure on your joints as running or jogging. You will need walking shoes!

1 Put on your walking shoes, set the timer on your phone for one minute, and GO!

2 Walk at a fast pace that is comfortable for you. No jogging or running!

3 As you're walking, focus on your breath. Allow any thoughts that come into your mind to flow in and flow out, and keep bringing your attention back to your breath and the walk.

4 When your timer goes off, STOP! Notice how you feel. Do you feel calmer? Are you thinking more rationally?

5 Start walking back at a slower pace as you feel more relaxed from your power walk.

6 Repeat throughout your day—start by doing a brisk one-minute walk and build up to two minutes, increasing your speed each time.

CONFLICT CHALLENGES

How you communicate is one of the main factors when it comes to dealing with conflict challenges. There can be situations at work, with friends, or with family that cause stress and frustration, especially when the other person doesn't see something from the same perspective as you. The more agitated or angry you become, the worse the outcome, as neither of you can agree on a solution that works for you both. Finding a resolution can be challenging if neither party is willing to back down.

If a person or situation is upsetting you, such as your boss at work, your partner, friend, or colleague, or perhaps you are being treated with disrespect and someone is constantly saying things to undermine you, these two instant micro meditations (see below and opposite) will help you in difficult moments.

micro meditation
SEE THINGS IN BLACK AND WHITE

This quick and simple micro meditation will give you the mental power to stop others from zapping you of your energy and take away their ability to hurt you anymore.

1 If a person or situation is upsetting you, such as your boss at work, your partner, friend, or colleague, instead of seeing them in full color, imagine turning the person or situation into black and white.

2 Now make the black and white fuzzy until it is barely noticeable anymore.

3 Notice how the person or situation has become totally insignificant and their attitude not worth wasting your energy on.

micro meditation

FOCUSING ON FUNNY CHARACTERS

This micro meditation has had many of my clients laughing in meetings or different situations at work or socially and has helped them feel much more in control of their emotions.

1 Imagine a cartoon character you think is funny.

2 See the person that is upsetting you become this character, and when they speak, imagine they are speaking in the same voice as the character you have chosen!

3 Notice how this powerful micro meditation weakens the other person's ability to intimidate and hurt you in the present moment.

quack! quack!

Keep practicing! The more you do the micro meditations in this book, the quicker they will come to you in the moment and you will feel much more in control.

REAL LIFE STORY
WEDDING PLANS CONFLICT

Lenny wasn't asked to be an usher at his sister Sally's wedding. Although they were best friends, Lenny felt left out, treated like one of the guests, and humiliated that he wasn't involved in any way. Arguments started between them and eventually they stopped speaking.

When Lenny came to see me, he was very upset and needed to take control of his emotions. He focused on the Count and Breathe in Stressful Moments micro meditation (see page 49) for a couple of minutes along with the Release Your Anxiety micro meditation (see page 18). The micro meditations helped him think more rationally as he calmed down. When Lenny felt more in control of his emotions, we talked about why he thought he had been left out. He realized that he hadn't given his sister or her fiancé an opportunity to explain and hadn't told them how he was feeling.

After our session, he sent his sister a letter explaining how he felt. The following day, Sally called him and asked to meet in their favorite coffee shop near their home. Sally explained she had no idea he was so upset—she wanted him to have fun with his girlfriend at the wedding. She thought he would be happy to be free of responsibility during the event and couldn't understand why he was so moody and argumentative with her. Lenny was so relieved. He had thought she didn't care and now realized she was only thinking of him!

Following their heart-to-heart, Lenny was made head usher. It was a beautiful wedding. Sally was very proud of how her brother organized everything and Lenny was so happy to have an important role with responsibility. He was beaming with happiness and had the best time!

Lenny continues to use his micro meditations. If he experiences conflict with anyone at work or home, they help to bring him back into the present moment and look at things more realistically.

In many situations where there is conflict, listening to why the other person doesn't agree with you can help you understand how they are feeling too. Maybe you haven't clarified your needs to them in a way that they can understand. Reframing how you are putting your point across in a calmer, more positive way can help you both come to an agreement. Remember, talking about and sharing your feelings can help you understand the other person's thoughts too. In the case study opposite, Sally just wanted Lenny to have fun and didn't tell him. Lenny thought she didn't care! By talking, they resolved the conflict. Always keep the doors of communication open to help avoid situations like Sally and Lenny's, or any other life challenges. Your micro meditations will let you rationalize your emotions in the moment, just as they did for Lenny.

RELATIONSHIP CHALLENGES THAT TEST YOU!

All relationships can put you to the test if you allow them! Family members can often be challenging and friends, colleagues, or your partner may also test you at different times.

- Special occasions can sometimes be stressful for everybody involved.

- Your siblings always seem to disagree with what you are doing and want to interfere.

- Your partner disapproves of how you look and wear your hair, the friends you hang out with, or the job you love.

- Your parents don't agree with your choice of partner and make it very difficult for you to include them in family occasions.

Whatever it is, you may notice that when friends and family test your patience, you feel like you're about to burst and say something you don't want to! When this happens, it's up to you how you react. Try the Anchor Away Your Frustrations micro meditation (see page 40), as well as the Eating Mindfully micro meditation (see page 92), to discover how you can change your focus in a moment when things get too heated!

micro meditation
ANCHOR AWAY YOUR FRUSTRATIONS

Anchoring is a powerful, grounding micro meditation that changes your mood in a moment with a tiny trigger—squeezing your thumb and forefinger together—which will help you to connect with a past, happy, soothing, positive memory and bring it into the present.

1 Think of a time that you felt calm and relaxed. You may be feeling happy and peaceful on holiday, enjoying the sounds of the gentle waves, the smell of sunscreen, lying on a sun lounger, and reading your favorite book with your favorite mocktail or cocktail! Imagine being there right now as though you've stepped into the moment. Feel what you were feeling.

2 Close your eyes and take a slow, deep breath in through your nose and slowly out through your mouth. Now, squeeze your thumb and forefinger together on one hand. This will be your future trigger to bring on this calm, relaxing memory in a moment.

3 Make the picture you see bigger, brighter, and bolder. Double and triple this feeling and enjoy this heightened moment of calm and peace. Imagine hearing yourself speaking calmly. Turn the volume up and hear yourself sounding relaxed and in control of your emotions.

4 Take a slow, deep breath in through your nose and out through your mouth and open your eyes.

5 Whenever a situation arises where you need to avoid shouting, screaming, or saying something you'll regret, just squeeze your thumb and forefinger together and your anchor will magically appear as you feel calmer and more relaxed in a moment!

Coping with Pain Physically and Mentally

I am a big advocate of holistic and traditional medicine working side by side when necessary. However, mindfulness and meditation are key factors in helping you manage different types of pain, including chronic pain. When you are coping with pain—whether physical or mental—your mind is the most powerful tool you have. It won't take away the pain, but it helps you to have a different relationship with it and how you see it.

Practicing micro meditations throughout your day will help you to manage your pain. It will remind you that you are in control, and you can manage it. Living with chronic pain can have a huge impact on your lifestyle if you let it but by accepting change and focusing on micro meditation regularly, your life can still be fun, happy, and positive. What you tell yourself has a massive impact on your unconscious mind and changing your self-talk (see pages 58–63), Positive Affirmations (see pages 64–65), and embracing nature (see pages 74–87) can also help.

REAL LIFE STORY
MY OWN EXPERIENCE OF COPING WITH PAIN

Since surviving a brain tumor operation in 2002, I have been left with chronic pain in my head. At first, I just wanted to crawl under a blanket and hide. I found it very challenging taking care of my children who were 13 and 16 years old. My then-partner bought me a shih tzu puppy and we called him Lucky. He wouldn't stop jumping on me, licking me, and demanding my attention. I adored him and so did my children. Lucky gave me a new lease of life.

I had to learn to walk and talk again as well as manage the pain. I started to focus on telling myself I could do this. I began doing micro meditations throughout the day, including focusing on my breath and repeating Positive Affirmations (see pages 64–65) to myself every morning when I woke up and during the day and evening when I needed to. The words "I'm in control of you, you're not in control of me" helped me to manage my pain. The more I said them the more they became embedded in my subconscious mind.

It took about six months after my operation to take Lucky to the woods and park and be able to call him. It was wonderful I could speak again— and I haven't stopped since! The micro meditations have changed my world, and I hope they can help to change yours, too, whatever your challenges may be.

DISAPPOINTED AND LET DOWN

There are all kinds of situations in your personal and work life where it can come as a shock when you are suddenly let down and disappointed, especially if you have been feeling happy and content.

- You were hoping to be promoted at work and your colleague beat you to it.

- You didn't get the apartment you had wanted that was near the beach.

- The relationship you have been in for a few years has ended as it didn't work out the way you both thought it would.

- A friend is moving away, and you had no idea; you feel hurt, upset, and let down that they didn't even talk to you about it.

Different emotions, such as hurt, anger, loss, sadness, and depression, can affect you and micro meditations will help you manage these emotions in the moment as you work through and process the experience.

BREAKUPS THAT HURT!

When a relationship hasn't worked out and your partner has decided it's over, it can be so heartbreaking. It's natural to feel all kinds of emotions when you break up with someone, especially after being in a long-term relationship and if you had no idea it wasn't working for your partner. Wondering why and what you did wrong can leave you in tears and devastated.

For whatever reason the relationship didn't work, it takes time to heal from a breakup and it's important to give yourself the headspace to feel better. In times of disappointment and upset it's easy to curl up into a ball and sit in front of the television, eat ice cream, and grieve for what you realize wasn't right. The Tub of Ice Cream micro meditation (see opposite) can help, as can tapping into your individual senses of touch, sight, sound, smell, and taste (see pages 88–97) or any of the crystal and chakra meditations (see pages 116–139).

micro meditation
THE TUB OF ICE CREAM

Just a spoonful of ice cream is absolutely the best medicine you can have if you're feeling upset or sad, or need a boost. This is a fabulous micro meditation that even Bridget Jones (a character played by Renee Zellweger in the well-known and very popular movie *Bridget Jones Diary*) indulged in. Many of us can relate to the emotionally challenging times she faced at various points during the movie, and ice cream was one of her go-to comforters, along with her diary. There are also many scenes in the sitcom *Friends* where they sit eating out of a huge tub of ice cream. It's like their own special micro meditation and I love this!

A little bit of indulgence for a couple of minutes every so often throughout your day is okay in moderation and the wonderful thing about ice cream is that it is delicious, as well as a comforting distraction! After the first few spoonfuls, it's amazing how all your emotions fade into the background and your focus becomes the delicious taste of chocolate, mint, fudge, coffee, or strawberry. There are so many different flavors to choose from and there are dairy-free options available too (or a tub of sorbet would be the perfect alternative if you prefer).

1 Always keep a tub of ice cream in your freezer at home or work and make sure to have a dessertspoon nearby.

2 When you feel you need a pick-me-up comforter, grab your spoon and your ice cream (or sorbet) from the freezer, sit on a comfortable chair or sofa, and give yourself a large spoonful of your favorite treat.

3 Take your time, noticing the texture and flavor on your tongue and savor the taste of each spoonful. The slower, the better, as you delight in every moment of your delicious indulgence.

4 Enjoy the feel-good factor!

REAL LIFE STORY
OLIVIA'S PICK-ME-UP BOOSTERS

Olivia had been looking forward to a meeting with her boss to discuss a new idea. At the last minute her boss let her down and cancelled—she had forgotten a prior engagement with a friend from out of town that wasn't in her diary. She apologized and said she'd rearrange soon. Olivia had wanted the meeting to be perfect and had spent hours planning and preparing her business idea. She felt very disappointed and let down. During the day she did several different micro meditations to help her.

Olivia ate several spoonfuls of ice cream from a huge tub (see previous page), counted backward from ten (see opposite), and focused on five things in her room which distracted her (see page 90). In less than two minutes these techniques helped Olivia change her mindset and gave her the confidence to go and see her boss the following day.

Oliva's boss agreed to meet Olivia that afternoon. It was such a successful meeting, she was asked to present her idea to the board. They also loved the idea! Now, every time Olivia feels disappointed or let down in her business or personal life, she always uses one of her micro meditations in the moment to help her get back control and feel better.

Time-Pressured Situations

Having a routine—like cleaning your teeth, getting dressed, and having your first hot drink of the day—can be wonderful, most of the time. It can give you a sense of purpose to get up in the morning and know what you are doing and when. There are occasions when it is almost a relief not to have the pressure of doing something or being somewhere at a particular time. It's such a good feeling to go to bed at night and know you don't have to put the alarm on—although this may not be the case if you know you're going to get woken up by little ones jumping on you at 6am every day (along with your dog or cat if you have animals too)! However, there are so many occasions when we can feel under time pressure.

- A routine for your children from first thing in the morning until bedtime can put so much pressure on you, especially if you don't get them to school on time or give them their dinner or bath when you planned.

- Work deadlines, too, are challenging if you're not in the right headspace to manage them. If you're struggling, this can turn into panic when you have looming deadlines and things don't get done on time.

- There are times you may get stuck in a situation that is completely out of your control, such as your computer crashing, your photocopier getting jammed, or you're late to teach a class.

Time pressure can bring on anxiety. It's important to stop and take a couple of minutes to put yourself into a relaxed space, so you can look at things objectively and find solutions. Micro meditations will give you the space to turn off the alarm in your head and realize that everything will get done, especially when you stop and reassess the situation.

Taking a slow, deep breath in and a slow breath out and then slowly counting backward from 10 out loud or to yourself will bring you back into the present moment and help you to manage your situation. See page 49 for another mini meditation you can do, which is counting with breathwork.

REAL LIFE STORY
CALI'S TIME-PRESSURED SOLUTION

Cali was on her way to teach a dance class and roadworks were preventing her from getting to the fitness studio on time. She started to panic as her class started in 20 minutes and her satnav said she was still 25 minutes away! In the moment Cali took a slow, deep breath in through her nose and slowly out through her mouth and started to count backward from 10. It brought her back into the present and helped her to realize that worrying just made things worse. There was nothing she could do.

Now she was thinking rationally, she pulled over to the side of the road and called the studio to say she would be about ten minutes late. Thank goodness for cell phones! In an instant she felt more in control and wasn't panicking. Cali's deep breathing and counting meditation changed how she was feeling in an instant. Her students were happy to see her when she arrived and had been concerned whether she was okay. They all had a fabulous dance class!

10 ... 9 ... 8 ... 7 ... 6 ...
5 ... 4 ... 3 ... 2 ... 1 ...

micro meditation
COUNT AND BREATHE IN STRESSFUL MOMENTS

Repeat this micro meditation regularly when you need to refocus. If you lose concentration, go back to the beginning and start counting from one.

1 Take a slow, deep breath in through your nose and slowly out through your mouth.

2 Now, with every slow breath in and every slow breath out, follow this micro meditation as you focus on your breath.

3 Silently in your mind, count 1 on your in breath and 2 on your out breath.

4 Count 3 on your in breath and 4 on your out breath.

5 Count 5 on your in breath and 6 on your out breath.

6 Count 7 on your in breath and 8 on your out breath.

Once you give yourself permission to stop and step out of the situation with a micro meditation, you will notice how much clearer your mind is and how much easier it is to manage your time-pressured situation. Think of who you can ask to help you if the photocopier paper gets caught. Ask a colleague if they can log into your account to access the document you need.

You can take the pressure off by choosing micro meditations such as focusing on your breathing (see page 17), tapping into your senses (see pages 88–97), face comforters (see page 104), or mindful eating (see page 92), which will give you some breathing space to decide the best thing to do.

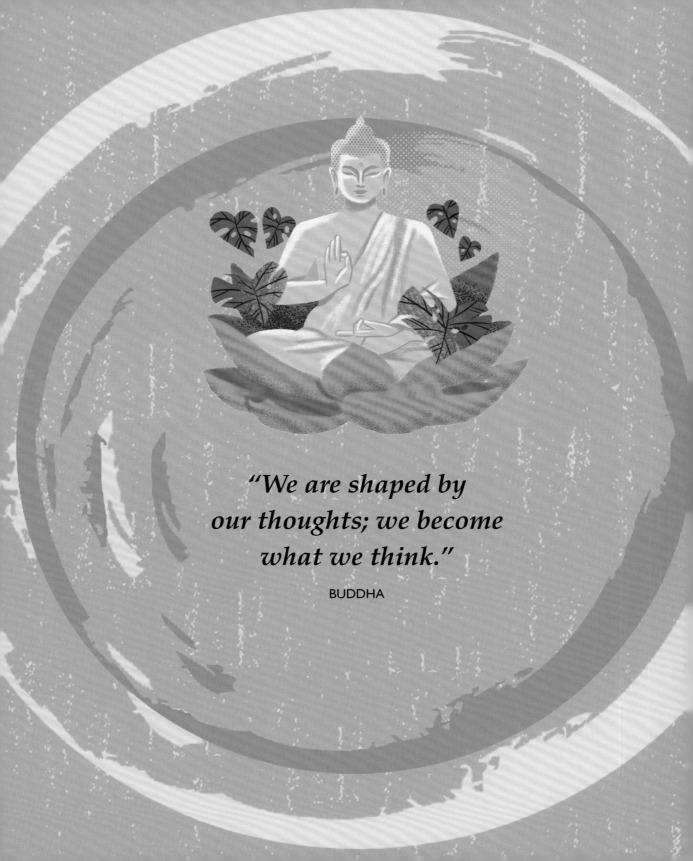

"We are shaped by
our thoughts; we become
what we think."

BUDDHA

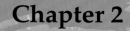

Chapter 2

Changing Your Mindset

Breaking a Negative Mindset

When you focus on the negative, you are constantly feeding your unconscious mind with negative thoughts.

The more you allow negativity to take over, the more it can affect your mental health and spiral into debilitating symptoms such as stress, anxiety, lack of confidence, and depression, which have a knock-on effect on your well-being. Having a negative mindset prevents you from being present in the moment and making the most of what you DO have. For example, perhaps you've started a healthy eating plan to get bikini fit for your vacation. After a few days there's no change, so you tell yourself it's not working and give up.

I CAN, I WILL, AND I WANT TO!

By retraining your brain with micro meditations, which change negative thoughts and words to positive ones, you are sending messages to your unconscious mind that will give you a new perspective on all you see and hear. Instead of giving up, you can be proud that you have started this new healthy regime—you know it will take a few weeks to kick in, but you will soon look and feel fabulous for your vacation!

Choosing to have a positive attitude can change your perception of any challenges going on in your life, from health or relationship issues to work or financial problems. Positivity will help enhance your mood, boost your energy and confidence, and shift your focus away from circumstances or people that may be pulling you down. Your mind and body will feel more energized and happier. A positive mindset has a huge effect on how you manage your day-to-day life and what you do to enhance it, giving a healthy balance and focus to all you do.

I'M PROUD OF MYSELF

Introducing daily micro meditations, and practicing them regularly throughout your day, can help you to break your negative cycle. It will take practice to make these changes something you're used to but by focusing on having a positive attitude, you will soon notice the shift in your mindset and how much better you feel with your new, positive focus. Positive Affirmations (see pages 64–65) will help you to focus on words that help you to feel good as you keep repeating them throughout your day. Positive Crystal Boosters (see page 118) will also help you change your negative mindset.

REAL LIFE STORY
ANNIE'S POSITIVE SHIFT

Annie owned several hair and beauty salons. One of the salons had a huge loss of income compared to the others and she had to close it down. Annie kept focusing on negative outcomes and worrying she would lose her other salons too, even though they were thriving and successful. She was so upset that she was having sleepless nights.

By changing her self-talk and introducing daily positive micro meditations into her life, Annie started to embrace what she did have. Every time she started to have negative thoughts she used her micro meditations to help. Her "What if?" became an excited "What now?" She was proud of all she had achieved and felt hopeful and excited about the future.

Being Grateful in the Moment

Focusing on being grateful in the moment can help you manage the small things that bother you every day. Even if you are stacking the dishwasher or tackling mountains of laundry, being grateful for everything you have changes your perspective in the moment and can help you feel less stressed as you realize how blessed you are.

When you focus on being grateful, you will find that it helps not only with the little things, but the big things, too. Gratitude, and seeing the positive side of things, can help you to calmly navigate life's ups and downs, from career changes to empty nest syndrome.

micro meditation
WHO AND WHAT ARE YOU GRATEFUL FOR IN LIFE?

As you go about your everyday life, take the time to look around and notice the things that perhaps many people usually take for granted. Perhaps the sun is shining outside, or you have work to do that you enjoy. Perhaps you are meeting friends or spending time with the special people in your life, or maybe you have a good book to curl up with this evening. Take the time to remind yourself how grateful you are for who and what is in your life—and remember to tell them how much you appreciate them! In the spaces below, note down five things in your life that you are grateful for:

1 I am grateful for ....

2 I am grateful for ....

3 I am grateful for ....

4 I am grateful for ....

5 I am grateful for ....

REAL LIFE STORY
ZOE'S STORY: FEELING GRATEFUL

Zoe has a full household of four teenage children. They are constantly demanding meals and snacks, leaving mess behind, running off to their room, or needing a lift to meet their friends. Zoe loves them all so much but emptying the dishwasher five times a day and tackling their mountains of laundry can become stressful, especially when she is also working full time. When everything becomes too much and overwhelm takes over (see page 22), Zoe reminds herself how grateful she is to have her beautiful children and a home with all the appliances she needs. She says being grateful, even when she's doing chores, brings her back into the moment and helps her to realize how lucky she is.

I AM LUCKY

I AM GRATEFUL

EMPTY NEST SYNDROME

When your kids leave home to go to college, move in with their partner, or live abroad, it can leave you feeling lost and empty. Life at home is suddenly quiet. There's no more mess, loud music, or piles of laundry! At first you may be feeling upset and then you realize how wonderful it is for your child to have this amazing opportunity and to become independent. After a while you notice how much more time you have to do things for yourself, instead of spending your days tidying up and cooking! Of course, you miss your child, but you suddenly have newfound freedom to explore.

Micro meditations can give you the clarity and motivation to look forward to things you aren't sure about, such as embracing new challenges in a positive way and telling yourself:

- "I'm looking forward to new beginnings."

- "I'm excited to start my new beauty course."

- "This is going to be a special time."

REAL LIFE STORY
LIVING YOUR LIFE WHEN THEY LEAVE HOME

Nancy was dreading the day her youngest son, Mark, went to college. She knew how much she would miss him and didn't know how she would cope. She was hoping he would attend a college nearby, so he could continue to live at home, but Mark wanted to study law and was hoping to go to the prestigious Yale University that his grandfather went to. When the results came through, Mark was so happy—he got his first choice! But while his dreams were coming true, Nancy was in tears.

When Nancy came to see me, she was so upset. She focused on comforting herself with some of the nurturing moments micro meditations, including the Face Comforter (see page 104) and Hand Massage micro meditation (see page 112). When I asked her to reframe her negative thoughts and look at the positives, Nancy began to realize how wonderful this was for Mark. Yale was only a plane ride away and he would still come home in the holidays. She also realized she would have more time to do things for herself, instead of always worrying about what Mark wanted.

Mark comes home for every holiday and Nancy makes sure they have regular video calls and daily texts. She also started going to the gym regularly, meeting up with friends, and having many more date nights with her husband. Mark is doing well and Nancy is very proud of him. Even though she misses him, she's enjoying her newfound freedom!

Changing Your Self-Talk

Your inner voice is your biggest critic. Your internal monologue has a huge impact on your daily life. Your brain absorbs these messages and they become a prominent part of how you feel and how you see yourself, how you talk to yourself and others, and how you react and behave in different situations. When you constantly allow yourself negative thoughts, your subconscious will react by continuing to send negative messages.

Research has shown how reframing self-talk from negative to positive can have a profound impact on your mental and physical health. As soon as you change what you are saying to the positive, you will find it easier to manage your well-being and any physical or mental pain you may be experiencing (see page 42), which will give you a new outlook on everything you do in your daily life. Practice and repetition will allow your positive thoughts to become embedded in your subconscious instead of the negative. These positive thoughts will then become your main focus and help you feel so much better.

micro meditation
REWRITE YOUR INNER DIALOGUE

Sometimes you may not even realize that you focus on negative self-talk. It may have become a regular habit but can cause upset and hurt to family, friends, and colleagues, as well as your own self-worth and self-belief. Thankfully, reframing your mindset is an instant micro meditation that can give you a wonderful mental shift!

1 Think about the negative, inner dialogue you tell yourself. Write down three examples.

2 Look at what you have written down and think of good, happy things you can say instead. Change the words or sentences to positive ones (see box, below).

3 Continue to repeat these positive self-talk statements throughout the day—you can make this an instant micro meditation as part of your daily routine. For example, keep a photo of your statements on your phone and look at your positive changes for 30 seconds at any time during your day or evening.

4 You may find these statements challenging initially but the more you practice, the easier they will be to incorporate into and become part of your subconscious.

NEGATIVE INNER DIALOGUE	POSITIVE INNER DIALOGUE
"I can't do it"	"I can have fun doing something new"
"I look terrible" or "I'm ugly"	"I love who I am" or "I'm beautiful inside and out"
"No one cares about me" or "No one likes me"	"I am cared for and loved" or "I'm happy I have friends that care about me"
"I'm so fed up"	"I'm going to do something fun"

micro meditation
REFOCUSING YOUR INTENTIONS FOR A HAPPY OUTCOME

Feeling how grateful you are for what you have, what you do, and what you are going to be doing will refocus your intentions and have a positive impact on your mindset.

1 Think about the things that are getting you down lately or making you feel stressed and anxious. Write them down.

2 Look at your list and think about the opportunities that doing these things can open up for you (see box, below).

3 Continue to repeat your new intentions throughout the day. Turning your positive intentions into regular micro meditations will help you to work through challenging emotions and look forward to the future.

NEGATIVE THOUGHTS	POSITIVE THOUGHTS
"I will miss hanging out with my friends at the beach"	"I can't wait to see my family" and "I can't wait to spend time with my niece and nephew"
"I will miss the sunny weather"	"I love walking in the woods by my home, hearing the rustle of the autumnal leaves, and feeling the autumn wind and sun on my face"
"I feel nervous about being a manager"	"I'm so excited to have my own team"

REAL LIFE STORY
LIZ'S SUMMER BUBBLE

Liz was working in Spain during the summer months. She had a fun time, made new friends, and enjoyed the sunny weather and laid-back lifestyle. When Liz's boss asked her to come home in mid-September, she wasn't happy. She'd forgotten how she had longed for a promotion and to head up her own team in the UK. The thought of coming home to autumnal weather and no beach bars filled her mind with negative thoughts and made her feel anxious and stressed.

During our online session, Liz talked about what she really wanted, such as career progression and a pay rise. Her family was also in the UK. She started to look at the positive aspects of coming home and, as she wrote them down, they far outweighed the negatives she had been telling herself. Plus, she remembered all she loved and had dreamed of (see micro meditation, opposite).

Liz reframed her outlook on life. She had been in a bubble for three months and now it was time to come home and do what she had always wanted. She flew home a couple of weeks early to prepare for the exciting new challenge of having her own team at work, being with her family, and enjoying the seasonal change!

Turning her positive affirmations into regular micro meditations helped Liz to work through her challenging emotions and made her stronger and more positive. Now, when a negative thought creeps in, she tells it "NO! I'm in control now and I feel good!"

DISTANCE YOURSELF FROM NEGATIVITY

Many of us struggle with emotional issues, which can prevent us from moving forward in life. We may want to have a successful career or meet the partner of our dreams but obstacles such as lack of confidence, negative self-belief, or focusing on negative outcomes can often get in our way. Micro meditations can give you clarity, boost your confidence, and help you manage situations differently. Helpful micro meditations include anchoring (see page 40), changing negative self-talk to positive (see page 59), and releasing anxiety (see page 18).

When you want to keep negativity at bay, it's a good idea to distance yourself mentally from the situation or person causing the problem. There are also times when we may not look at a situation as it really is, and instead jump to conclusions. Take a breath and give the other person an opportunity to show you that your thoughts weren't correct.

The following micro meditation (see opposite) will help you to create your own mental space without anyone else's negative energy affecting you. It will help you to imagine whatever is troubling you as being far away, rather than holding on to a feeling that is upsetting you and making you anxious or stressed. Changing your self-talk constantly will give you that instant, feel-good boost.

micro meditation
GIVE YOURSELF HEADSPACE

I love this exercise because it's simple and very effective in helping you to create mental space for yourself. You can do it anywhere and at any time, as needed. Do it discreetly and say the words in the steps to yourself instead of out loud if you're with other people.

1 Put your left hand on your heart and say out loud (or discreetly to yourself if you're in company): "I'm taking care of me."

2 Push your right hand straight out in front of you and focus on it.

3 Imagine you are pushing the person or situation farther and farther away as you say out loud: "And you're over there."

4 Repeat this 8–10 times.

5 Each time you speak, be aware of the space between you and whoever or whatever it is you're putting "over there." Feel how much more you're gaining control over your emotions and feeling clearer and happier in your mind.

6 Feel yourself relax and take a slow, deep breath in through your nose and out through your mouth as you release any tension you were holding on to.

7 Once you feel you have created the space between you and the person or situation you want to distance yourself from, you can replace the words "And you're over there" with 'This is your issue, not mine." This will help you feel much more in control of your emotions moving forward now you have created the headspace you needed.

Positive Affirmations

Positive affirmations are an excellent feel-good daily practice. As a micro meditation, these empowering words can bring you into the present moment, and the more you use them, the more they will become embedded in your unconscious mind.

It's important to choose words that resonate with how you feel. You may have different affirmations for different situations—choosing words that empower you in certain scenarios will train your brain to focus on positive thoughts when you need them. You might choose to say them out loud or quietly to yourself depending on where you are! Here are some positive affirmations that may resonate with you:

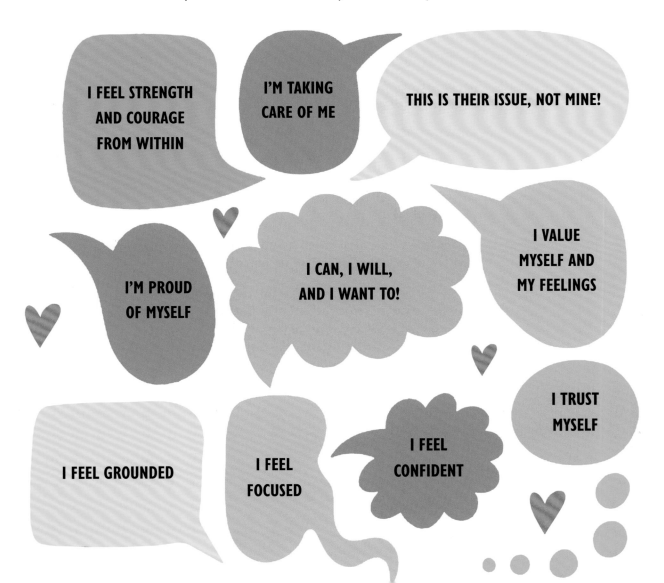

REAL LIFE STORY
THAT WAS THEN, THIS IS NOW

One evening Angie went with a group of friends to a nightclub she hadn't been to before. They were all having fun, dancing, laughing, and enjoying themselves, but when her friends started dancing with other people, Angie was left standing at the bar on her own. The following week her friends invited her out again. She said she didn't feel well, but the truth was, she didn't want to be left in that situation again.

THAT WAS THEN, THIS IS NOW

After talking through what had happened in her therapy session with me, she realized her friends weren't to blame. They were just having fun and didn't mean to leave her out, and she felt reassured that she could have joined in. To encourage Angie to go to the nightclub again, I encouraged her to repeat the positive affirmation "That was then, this is now," then add "It's going to be a fun night!" This mini micro meditation brought Angie back into the present moment and gave her the confidence to have a great evening. She had such fun and even met someone to dance the night away with!

The first time I walked into a wedding reception on my own many years ago, it wasn't something I felt comfortable doing. I didn't know anyone apart from the bride at the time, but I was excited for my friend—I wanted to be there and was determined not to let my discomfort ruin it for me. I took a deep breath and told myself: "I feel really excited and happy to be here," "I'm looking forward to meeting the bride's friends and family," and "It's going to be a fabulous day." In moments, this worked wonders for my self-esteem! I had a huge smile on my face and had the best time.

Sometimes we need to take that leap of faith; to trust and believe in ourselves and what we can do. I've never looked back and have felt confident to walk into a room without knowing anyone—sometimes a thousand people or more—ever since. These positive affirmations are so empowering and very motivating.

Boost Your Confidence and Manage Nerves

Maybe you're about to stand up and give a talk to a roomful of people and feel self-conscious about how you come across to others. Perhaps you're going to an interview for a job you really want. Going on a first date can also be exciting and daunting at the same time! There may be questions running through your mind such as:

"Will they like me?"

"Will I like them?"

"What do I talk about?"

"What shall I wear?"

Focusing on being present can help you to relax and feel calm. There are lots of mindfulness micro meditations that can help you, including breathing and counting (see page 49) and Positive Affirmations (see page 64–65). If you're lacking confidence, the nerves have set in, and your anxiety is rising, the Step Into Your Positive micro meditation (see page 68) will cool you down and help you feel your confidence come through in less than two minutes.

REAL LIFE STORY
STEP INTO YOUR INSPIRATION LIKE FRANK

Frank was a tall, strong, and very powerful super rugby league player. He was quite shy—after his games, he never spoke at any of the events or to the media when his team won. When I started working with the team to give them techniques that would help them focus on the pitch and boost their confidence when talking to the media, I asked them: "Who inspires you and why?" To the amazement of his fellow team members, Frank stood up and said "Arnie Schwarzenegger!"

Frank explained that, as he was walking down the tunnel to the pitch, he imagined stepping into Arnie's character in the *Terminator* movies. He said this made him feel confident and positive and couldn't wait to get out on the pitch and score.

After working with Frank, he became one of the main team members to speak to the press regularly as he felt so much happier and more confident in himself.

Manifest Instant Change

Since surviving a brain tumor in 2002, I look forward to going to the hairdressers once a week to alleviate the tension in my head with a wonderful hair wash and head massage. I have three plates and six screws in my head—one of which is loose—and since having my brain tumor operation, I have had a head massage every week. It's my special "me time!" Whenever I go there, I need a parking space, and I get the same spot every time—it's magical!

As I'm driving to the spot I want to be in, I imagine seeing the car parking space, and going straight into it. I say "Thank you" as though I have already received the space.

micro meditation
MANIFEST IN A MOMENT

This wonderful, quick, and simple mini manifestation meditation helps me to feel relaxed.

1 When you're not achieving an immediate goal, take a moment to focus on it. Visualize seeing it in your mind's eye.

2 Imagine having received it. The secret here is really believing you have already received what you want.

3 Feel grateful and happy—and remember to say "Thank you!"

Have a go with small things, like imagining receiving a text message or phone call from a friend you haven't heard from in a long time or being asked out on a date by someone you like.

There are many ways to manifest your dreams (both small and big) and you can find out how in my book *Manifest Your Everything*. However, if you want to manifest something quickly with a mini meditation, try the micro meditation below.

"Let nature's breathtaking gifts
bring you peace, calm, and happiness,
each and every day."

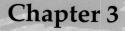

Chapter 3

Finding Your Calm

Embracing Nature's Distractions

The most beautiful gift you can give yourself is spending time in nature. Being outside can have a positive impact on you in many ways, both physically and mentally, and is wonderful for your overall well-being. Just a few of the benefits include:

- Improving your mood.

- Reducing anxiety, stress, or anger.

- Relaxing you.

- Giving you a boost of confidence.

When life is busy at work and/or at home, it's easy to find excuses not to step outside into this magical, natural world and just breathe. There are many micro meditations that can help you to embrace nature and feel good. The micro meditations on the following pages (see pages 76–87) use the distractions of nature to benefit you in every season of the year and will give you the peace and clarity you may be looking for.

SPRING

Spring is a time for blossom on the trees, bunny rabbits hopping around the backyard, and animals coming out of hibernation. The weather is warmer, flowers are blooming, and there is a beautiful fragrance in the air. It's such a relief to have lighter mornings and longer days. I always love this time of year, when the grass is bright green again after the winter months and it's time to make daisy chains or hold buttercups under your chin to see if you like butter!

It's also the perfect time to give your home a good spring clean and cleanse everything around you. Springtime clears the head, giving you the space to come up with new ideas. Micro meditations, such as The Fragrance of Spring (see opposite) and Bring Nature Into Your Home (see page 78), can help you to refuel your mind and body after the dark, cold days of winter and emerge with a renewed energy and vitality.

micro meditation

THE FRAGRANCE OF SPRING

I've always loved the delicate fragrance of freesias. These pretty flowers are said to symbolize friendship, which is beautiful, and they can be found all over the world. When you're walking in the park or woods, this season's floral micro meditation will help put the spring back into your step!

1 If you catch the beautiful scent of spring flowers in the air, look around and focus on finding the one you love.

2 Take a slow, deep breath in through your nose and slowly breathe out through your mouth.

3 Repeat several times. Allow the fragrance to fill you with nature's best natural medicine, which will heal and give you what you need, stimulate your senses, and lift your mood in an instant.

BRING NATURE INTO YOUR HOME

Lavender is a wonderful relaxant, especially before bed. In moderation, it will help you have a restful night's sleep (but avoid too much as it can also be a stimulant). If you have a lot on your mind, it also helps to lift your mood and release anxiety, and can help with insomnia.

1 There are many simple ways to bring the calming sensations of the seasons into your home and ensure you are rested and revitalized. For example:

  • Keep lavender flowers outside your bedroom.

  • Invest in a small, lavender-scented pillow.

  • Add a drop of lavender essential oil blended with coconut or almond oil to your pillow.

2 At any time during your day or when you get home after a busy day at work, close your eyes and breathe in the soothing aroma of lavender to give you a few moments of calm.

3 Enjoy this wonderful scent just enough to take the edge off your hectic schedule and relax you without falling asleep!

SUMMER

Summer is the time to enjoy all you have prepared for during the months of spring! The sun shining brightly against a blue sky and the wonderful heat on your face not only gives you a boost of Vitamin D, but also a burst of energy, and you feel so much more alert and happy!

Summer is seen as holiday time for many, especially if you have kids on vacation. It's the season of fun and laughter, having fun with friends or your partner, playing with your kids on the beach or by the pool, and taking some "me time" to relax and revitalize. Reading a book, flicking through magazines, or listening to your favorite music is a great distraction to take your mind off different situations that have been bothering you.

The summer season is also the time for even more outdoor activities as more cyclists and runners are outside exercising, while ice cream is for sale on every street corner to cool you down on a hot summer's day.

micro meditation
SUMMER NIGHTS

If you need some instant summer magic, this micro meditation will give you a couple of minutes to step out of any emotional turmoil you are going through and into a place that makes you smile and feel happy and carefree.

1 Take a moment to switch off your thoughts and just breathe in the summer air.

2 Imagine feeling the warm breeze on your face, enjoying the smell of the ocean, and hearing friends laughing and having fun.

3 Think of a happy, summer song you like. Play it in your head or put on your headphones; listen, sing along, and dance in the moment.

FALL

There's something magical about the fall. Walking in the woods or the park is so special at this time of year. Fall leaves in all their colors are so stunning when you see the orange, yellow, red, and brown shades on the trees and ground. It has a wonderful aura that makes you smile and feel as if you're inside a beautiful picture. The days get shorter and darker as the clocks go back, giving us an extra hour's rest, which is always a good thing!

micro meditation
FALL CELEBRATION

Fall is a particularly special time of year for celebrating with events like Thanksgiving and harvest festival to look forward to. This micro meditation offers you the chance to be grateful and give blessings for all you have in your life.

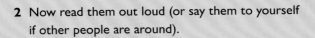

1 Write down three things you want to celebrate that you have achieved during your year.

• ....

• ....

• ....

2 Now read them out loud (or say them to yourself if other people are around).

3 Take a photo on your phone, so you can keep reminding yourself of the blessings you have in your life.

micro meditation
A WALK IN THE WOODS OR PARK

This is a favorite micro meditation that I like to suggest to my clients and students. I also love doing this with my grandsons, who have great fun kicking the leaves as though they are a football! It's a wonderful and freeing feeling.

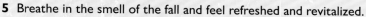

1 The next time you are walking in the woods or park, indulge your senses.

2 Listen to the crunching of the fall leaves under your feet.

3 Embrace feeling carefree and happy as you kick the leaves and have fun throwing them in the air.

4 Enjoy the beauty of the colors of the leaves on the trees and all around you.

5 Breathe in the smell of the fall and feel refreshed and revitalized.

WINTER

When I think of winter, a picture comes into my mind of pure white snow, sparkling in the sunshine on a cold winter's day. I love seeing the footprints from my snow boots as I walk through the thick, freshly fallen snow and listen to the silence around me. The air is fresh, cold, and so invigorating. I'm also drawn to the smell of roasted chestnuts in the town center. They are delicious!

It's very special to sit outside on winter evenings. Wrap up in a warm, cozy blanket, watch the dancing flames of a burning log fire, drink hot chocolate topped with marshmallows, and enjoy the moment. Any worries or upset you are feeling will flow away. If you have never done this, try the micro meditation opposite.

Winter is a time of reflection and can be a challenging time for many. As festivities approach and everyone is focused on gifts and celebrations for the holidays, missing loved ones and grieving for those who have passed can be painful. Remembering happy times and reaching out to talk can help you manage your pain and give you comfort.

micro meditation
A CUP OF WINTER COMFORT

Focus your attention on the details of this micro meditation to take your mind away from negative energy you don't want. Notice how each step gives you a different focus—just adding the marshmallows is a micro meditation on its own! Notice how everything you do ultimately comes together so you can enjoy your drink.

A wonderful alternative to hot chocolate is cacao, which is cocoa in its purest form. You can buy it from most health food stores. It is rich in antioxidants and research shows it has fabulous health benefits, from reducing inflammation to boosting your energy. A cup of cacao is soothing and relaxing, and gives you a feeling of peace. I like to call it "calm in a cup." I've enjoyed many cacao ceremonies and included them in many meditation classes and workshops, including the well-being retreat Shanti-Som in Monda, Spain. It's very bitter, so you may like to add a spoonful of honey, agave, or whatever you prefer to sweeten the taste. You could also add oat milk or just enjoy hot water with a spoonful of cacao depending on your preference.

1 Make yourself a cup of hot chocolate, or another warm drink if hot chocolate isn't for you. Add marshmallows on top, slowly and one by one, being mindful as you place each one.

2 Wrap up in a warm coat, hat, and scarf and take your hot drink outside with you.

3 Focus on holding your mug with both hands, feeling the warmth, and enjoying the inviting aroma of your drink. Notice the cool air on your face.

4 Breathe in slowly through your nose and slowly out of your mouth.

5 Now sip your drink and enjoy it!

A TREE FOR ALL SEASONS

Nature's trees are magical and magnificent. They stand tall and proud, encompassing their surroundings and yet have a personality of their own, which changes with the seasons. In spring they blossom, emerging from the colder, darker months. In summer they are green and lush, and in the fall they are colorful and a joy to see. They shed their beautiful coat of leaves in the winter, but continue to stand firmly with their roots in the ground. Trees have a wonderful energy that you can harness during your micro meditations.

micro meditation
FIND A SPECIAL TREE FOR YOU

Trees will give you a boost whenever you place your hands on them. This wonderful micro meditation will give you energy, clarity, and peace in the moment. It also grounds you, helping you to feel more balanced while you focus on the now.

1 When you're out walking in the park or woods, find a tree you are drawn to.

2 Notice how tall it is; see the color of the leaves or the bare branches depending on the season.

3 Place your hands on the tree and close your eyes.

4 Take a slow, deep breath in through your nose and slowly out through your mouth three times and then find a normal comfortable breath for you.

5 Stay here for 30–60 seconds. Feel the vibration and energy of the tree through your hands.

6 Take a slow, deep breath in through your nose and a slow breath out through your mouth.

7 Open your eyes and give your tree a hug! This feels so good!

Tapping Into Your Senses

Each of your five main senses—touch, sight, hearing, taste,
and smell—bring you into the present moment to distract
you from whatever is causing you stress, upset, or overwhelm.
It's important to focus on your senses regularly to heighten and
enhance them. Tapping into one of your wonderful senses at a time
for a couple of minutes or less throughout your day will help you
feel their positive impact, bring you into the present, and give you
the feel-good factor.

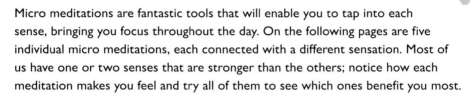

Micro meditations are fantastic tools that will enable you to tap into each
sense, bringing you focus throughout the day. On the following pages are five
individual micro meditations, each connected with a different sensation. Most of
us have one or two senses that are stronger than the others; notice how each
meditation makes you feel and try all of them to see which ones benefit you most.

TOUCH

Touch brings comfort and a beautiful sense of connection. You can feel its warmth
or vibrations. Being tactile—for example, by holding hands with someone or giving
yourself a hug—releases the love hormone oxytocin, which then releases
other feel-good hormones like dopamine and serotonin. Touch
changes your mood when you need a boost.

We experience touch through the many nerve receptors on our
skin, which enable us to feel different sensations. Different textures
can change your mood. Soft, fluffy blankets can be soothing and
cool water flowing over you in a shower can be invigorating.
From rough to smooth, soft to hard, cold to hot, or even
slimy, wet, and sticky, whatever you touch can change
your mindset in a moment. If you are feeling unwell or
suffering any pain, such as backache or neck ache,
the touch and feeling of a light massage on the
area, a hot-water bottle, or a cold compress
can relieve tension in an instant.

micro meditation
STOP AND TOUCH

When you need a sudden distraction, this simple touch meditation will take your mind away from any negative thoughts or worry. This is a mindful moment to release any tension and just relax!

1 Wherever you are stop and touch five different things.
   For example, if you're in your bedroom, you could touch your cool, cotton sheets, the soft, velvet fabric of your bed cushion, your textured rug on the floor, the sticky mark left on your nightstand, or the wax from a candle.

2 Keep your hand on each texture for 2–3 seconds.

3 As you do this, notice how the emotions you were feeling have shifted. This micro meditation opens your tactile senses and takes away any negative thoughts.

4 If necessary, repeat this 2–3 times.
   Go outside and touch a rough brick, the wet, sticky mud, or the cool rain with your fingertips. You could also have fun with this sense and touch different things like a wobbly jelly in your fridge or put your hands into a plate of pasta and feel the smooth, soft, wet texture!

SIGHT

Your sight is a gift that enables you to see the world in all its beautiful colors, shapes, and patterns. When you look into the eyes of loved ones, friends, or colleagues there is a sense of connection. Sight gives us the opportunity to observe others and see life in all kinds of situations. If you have a sight impairment, touch, hearing, taste, and smell can become your eyes, helping you to see the world in a different way. This micro meditation will bring you back into the present moment if you need to get what is bothering you out of your head and focus on different things.

micro meditation
LOOK AND FOCUS ON FIVE THINGS

If you suddenly feel your heart racing and panic sets in or you are unable to stop worrying and thinking of an upsetting situation, change your focus in an instant with this fabulous micro meditation distraction. Here's how to focus and look!

1 If you suddenly have a wave of emotion, look around you.

2 Choose five things to focus on.

3 Spend 2–3 seconds looking at each one.

4 Repeat a few times until you feel the wave of emotion disappear.

5 Take a slow, deep breath in through your nose and slow breath out through your mouth.

TASTE

Taste is a great sense to focus on with micro meditation. Your taste buds tell you if you're eating something sweet, sour, bitter, or salty. When you eat something indulgent, such as chocolate, cake, or cookies, the delicious flavor magically helps anything troubling you fade away in the moment because you immediately connect to the flavors and not the issue that is upsetting you. Whether you are an omnivore, vegetarian, or vegan, your taste buds will be stimulated by whatever you choose to eat.

micro meditation
TASTE, CONNECT, AND RESET

I believe that a little of something you love is good for you—everything in moderation gives us a balanced lifestyle. Keep this taste micro meditation nearby to use whenever you need it. If the phone keeps ringing and you're feeling overwhelmed by work or family pressures, simply stop and indulge in a few tasty moments!

1 Make a bag of treats containing five things that you love. For example, one piece each of sweet popcorn, milk chocolate, and dark chocolate, plus one raisin and a blueberry or strawberry to give you something fruity! Or perhaps you prefer savory foods, such as a cube of cheese, a mini square piece of pizza, one salt-and-vinegar or cheese-and-onion chip (crisp), one small pretzel, and a piece of salted popcorn.

2 Store the bag by your desk, in your bag, or wherever you may need it.

3 Every time you feel everything is getting too much, dip into your bag.

4 Enjoy the flavor of each treat individually for a few seconds. By doing this you will be diverting your attention away from everyday pressure and allowing yourself to reset.

5 Make up more bags of these treats for when you need them. Keep perishable items in a fridge at work or home, or if you're carrying the bag around with you, choose things that don't need refrigerating, like the sweet or salted popcorn.

micro meditation
EATING MINDFULLY

When the atmosphere is becoming overbearing at the dinner table, or the conversation is getting heated, this simple and effective micro meditation can give you the opportunity to slow down, bring you into the present moment, and provide you with headspace. Mindful or conscious eating is also wonderful for your digestion.

1 Take yourself out of the situation for a minute or two to eat mindfully.

2 Refocus your mind on what you are eating and how you eat it by engaging your sense of taste.

3 Eat slowly as you savor and chew every mouthful.

4 Enjoy this moment of calm as all the chatter and intense atmosphere around you clears from your mind and your concentration is completely on what you are eating.

Savor every mouthful, embrace every texture, and indulge yourself with wonderful tastes that bring you into the present moment while everything around you fades into insignificance.

SMELL

Lovely smells can give you a sense of comfort. Perhaps there is
a familiar aroma that makes you smile and remember happy times,
like your favorite perfume or food your grandmother made, which brings back
a special memory. This is known as your olfactory sense. Smell can also be very
unpleasant if there is a scent you don't like, such as a waft of waste coming from drains.
When my son was born, I took him for a walk in the pram every day. We had to pass
the fish dealer and the smell was awful; I had to cover my nose and mouth when we
went by. We always went to the park afterward, where the relief of the fresh air and
the scent of flowers and freshly cut grass was so much more appealing!

micro meditation
COMFORTING AROMAS

Different smells can affect your mood. If you're upset about a situation,
this olfactory micro meditation is the perfect comforter.

1 Collect five things that stimulate your olfactory senses and give you
a mood boost. For example:

- A scent of perfume you like. Spray on your wrists or on
a handkerchief, so you can sniff whenever you need to.

- The delicious aroma of chicken soup boiling on the stove. Put it
in a flask and enjoy smelling it—and probably drinking it too!—as
you unscrew the lid throughout your day.

- The smell of coffee beans is delicious, even if you're not a coffee drinker
like me! Keep a small bag of a few coffee beans.

- Perhaps you like the smell of fresh bread or a bag of candy, as it brings back
soothing memories from when you were a child.

2 Store the items in separate small bags and keep them nearby.

3 Smell in the moment to give you comfort when you need it.

4 Spend a few seconds with each of these special aromas, focus on the smells in the
moment, and enjoy the happy, comforting feeling they give you.

SOUND

If you wake up every morning to the sound of birds tweeting, dogs barking, cats meowing, rain pouring down outside your window, or your children laughing and chatting in the other room, it is a blessing. Being aware of sounds and their vibrations enables us to listen and engage with others.

Hearing, also known as your auditory sense, can invoke comforting memories. As a child, I remember the excitement every time my sister and I heard the ice cream truck's catchy tune in our road, encouraging us to run outside and buy an ice cream. We couldn't wait to get our pocket money and buy our Flake '99 (equivalent to a soft serve cone in the USA—just add the chocolate bar!)

Sound can also alert us to things we may need to hear, such as an alarm going off in our home or car, the smashing of a plate on the floor, or a gush of wind that throws open a window.

My father was deaf in one ear following a childhood ear infection. He learned how to manage it and always made sure he sat on the right side when talking with me … and the other side when he didn't want to listen to someone! There are varying degrees of hearing loss, from mild to complete deafness, and your other senses may be heightened even more to help you. Hearing aids, sign language, and lip reading are just a few of the magical wonders that can make life easier. It's important to let people know how mild or strong your hearing impediment is, so they can help you, especially if you're at an event and need to be nearer the front to hear the speaker.

micro meditation
LISTEN AND ENGAGE
WITH POSITIVE DISTRACTION

This auditory micro meditation enables you to switch off the noises and sounds you don't want to engage in and focus on the ones you do.

1 Take a slow, deep breath in through your nose and slowly out through your mouth. Find a comfortable breath for you and listen to the rhythm of your own, normal breath as you do this.

2 Pay attention to five sounds around you. What is the first sound you hear? For example:

- A car driving by.

- A cyclist tinkling their bell.

- Your kettle whistling as it boils.

- Bees buzzing around on a hot summer's day.

3 Whatever your five things are, embrace these sounds and focus on them by enjoying them one at a time. They are a wonderful distraction.

Take a moment to stop, breathe, and listen ...

Musical Moments

Music is magic and can change your mood in an instant. Dopamine, known as the pleasure chemical, is released when we hear songs we love; we connect to the melody and this has a positive impact on our mental well-being.

Music makes us feel happy or relaxed depending on what we listen to. It can help you if you're feeling anxious or worried (see Worry Wobbles, page 20) or elevate your mood if you're feeling sad and need an instant pick-me-up. Stressful or overwhelming times (see pages 22–31) may need immediate action to release the tension and calm your emotions. Keep your headphones nearby, so you can pop them in your ears and switch on your favorite song when needed. It will help to calm your senses in moments.

REAL LIFE STORY
MUSIC FOR ALL AGES

When I hear Julie Andrews sing "Do Rei Me" from *The Sound of Music* or "Just a Spoon Full of Sugar" from *Mary Poppins*, I sing along, too, and it makes me smile. When Michael Bublé sings "I'm Feeling Good," I feel good, too! I only have to hear Tom Jones sing the first two lines of "It's Not Unusual" and I'm transported to Tom Jones world. The sound of his voice makes me go weak at the knees, and everything else goes out of my mind in an instant!

My daughter Gemma has the most beautiful voice, and I could listen to her singing for hours. I love how she can soothe my grandson Charlie to sleep by singing him a lullaby. Once the children are in bed, after a long day of being with them both, she finds that making the dinner or washing up is the perfect excuse to sing her favorite songs. She even imagines the washing-up brush is her microphone! I asked Gemma how singing makes her feel and she said it helps her to switch off from the day; in a matter of moments, she's having her own special time and feels energized and relaxed.

I remember having fun with music when Gemma and my son Adam were little. We used a hairbrush as our microphone! Children need regular distraction as they can become frustrated if they aren't kept busy. Music is a huge distraction for my four grandsons, Louis, Charlie, Toby, and Jack. Charlie always throws his cookie on the floor if he wants attention, so I know it's time for Grandma to turn on the music and start dancing or play the drums! When they were babies, they all loved being sung the children's songs "Row the Boat," "The Wheels on The Bus," and "Baby Shark." It takes less than two minutes to change their mood from frustrated or upset to laughing and smiling.

If you have teenagers, their taste in music may be very different from yours. The excitement and popularity of popstars like Taylor Swift and Ed Sheeran, among many others, seem to capture the joy of music for teenagers and all ages. I think they're both fabulous too! If your teenager's music is not your "thing," I absolutely recommend putting headphones on and listen to what you love instead!

micro meditation
YOUR MUSICAL DISTRACTION

What music resonates with you? Which songs give you that feel-good buzz? Write down three tracks that make you feel happy and listen to them every time you need a positive boost.

1 ....

2 ....

3 ....

Whether you're listening to music, singing or humming along to your favorite song, dancing, or playing any kind of instrument, such as a guitar or piano, it is the ultimate distraction. In less than two minutes you, too, can feel as though you're transported to the world of music or to a place where you feel good!

If you want to get musical to elevate your mood in an instant and you're not sure how, here are a few tips to get you started:

- Start listening to different music, from pop to jazz, and see what gets you singing and dancing along!

- Break into song whenever you feel like it—in the shower, or when cooking or washing up. Have a go at singing with your washing-up brush, like my daughter (see page 99).

- Download a karaoke app on your phone or TV.

- Invest in a musical instrument. Maybe you've always wanted to learn to play an instrument such as the guitar or the piano. A two-minute rendition of "Chopsticks" or strumming a few chords on the guitar can bring you back into the present moment if you are worrying about a situation. It's very satisfying and feels good!

- Join a singing group at your local community center.

- "Do Rei Me" will always be my go-to song because it's fun, it's uplifting, and it takes you into a world of make-believe. The fabulous chorus is catchy and powerful, and has a wonderful vibration and energy. Repeat it three times to yourself or out loud depending on where you are. It will raise your vibrations and in less than two minutes give you a boost and put you in a better mood. "Three Little Birds" by Bob Marley is also one of the best music micro meditations when you are feeling worried and need reassurance that everything will be okay. The whole song, especially the chorus, is one of my favorites to sing along to and put a smile on everyone's face in my Manage Your Stress and Confidence workshops. If you have kids, they will love singing along, too, or perhaps you prefer to put your ear pods in.

Mini Mantras

The word "mantra" has different meanings depending on where you look. It is a Sanskrit word and the most simple and easiest meaning to remember is "sound." A mantra is a sound, word, or sentence that you chant over and over again, allowing its vibrations to resonate with your subconscious and distract you for as short or as long a time as you wish.

A word or sound, often used at the beginning and end of meditations, is the sacred mantra "Om," which is known as the universal sound, and is what the Hindu Sutras say is the sound of creation. It has a profound impact as a micro meditation as it can bring you back into the present. Chanting Om can help you feel calmer, happier, and healthier. It can also improve focus and concentration and help you reduce stress and anxiety.

The first time I chanted Om I was in Florida on a course with meditation guru Deepak Chopra. It was an incredible experience as the sound vibrated through my whole body. I felt completely calm and relaxed, and it gave me a sense of total peace from within. That night I slept so well and I always feel a surge of energy and enlightenment after chanting this word.

micro meditation
CHANT OM

"Om" is also spelt as A-U-M and is repeated a few times at the beginning and end of a traditional meditation. As you chant each "Om," allow this universal sound to resonate through your body and feel the wonderful vibrations flow through you.

1 Sit in a comfortable position with the palms of your hands on each thigh facing up.

2 Take a slow, deep breath in through your nose and, as you exhale, let the sound of "Om" come up from your diaphragm and flow out through your mouth. Feel the vibrations in your chest and throat, and on your lips.

3 Say "Om" several times and feel the vibrations going through your body as you notice how calm, peaceful, and uplifted you feel.

Nurturing Moments

On the following pages are five simple and effective micro meditations you can do in less than two minutes to help soothe and comfort you. The calming feeling this gives you is the perfect way to take you into your own world of relaxation and peace physically and mentally. Giving yourself these nurturing moments takes less than two minutes throughout your day to feel much better.

micro meditation
FACE COMFORTER

Stroking your own face can be one of the most soothing things to do when you are feeling different emotions such as upset, hurt, or anger.

1 With both hands, using the tips of two or three of your middle fingers, very slowly and gently massage your temples—the areas between your forehead and ear at the side of your eye—in a counterclockwise, circular motion.

2 Draw soft lines over your forehead with the tips of your fingers. As you do, take a deep breath in through your nose and slowly out through your mouth.

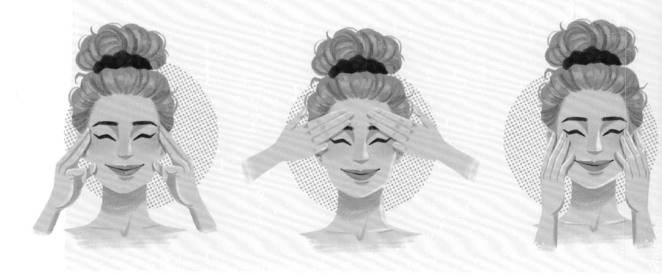

3 Starting from the top of your nose outward, gently brush light strokes over your eyelids with the tips of two or three fingers. Gently press just under your eyebrows three times as you go along your eyebrow. Press lightly down your face by the side of your eyes and coming under your eyes. Using the lightest touch, brush from underneath the corner of your eye outward with gentle, sweeping movements. Then repeat the process in reverse, working outward and back up to just under your eyebrow. Stay conscious of breathing slowly at the same time.

4 Draw gentle lines down the sides of your face. Repeat these downward strokes a few times for 10–20 seconds, depending on how you're feeling. Continue moving over to your cheeks in a slow, light motion as though you are gently tickling them.

5 Finally, slowly start brushing down over your lips and chin, from the top of your lips to the base of your chin, as you continue being conscious of your slow and relaxed breath. Feel the light, tingling sensation over your lips and chin.

6 This micro meditation will help you soothe away the tension you're feeling. As you begin to feel calmer, comforted, and more relaxed, sense any headache and tension start to release.

REAL LIFE STORY
SOOTHED LIKE A BABY

When my daughter Gemma was three months old, we were on a long-haul flight to America. She wouldn't stop crying and the flight attendant asked if she could have a go at comforting her. She started to gently stroke Gemma's face (see Face Comforter on page 104), and within moments Gemma was calm and fell asleep! I was delighted and so were the other passengers. It's something that's always stayed with me and has become one of my favorite go-to micro meditation soothers for children and adults.

micro meditation
RELIEVE AND RELAX JAW TENSION

So many people tend to hold tension around the jawline. Your worry, anxiety, and life challenges may result in you clenching your teeth during the day without you realizing it or grinding them at night when you sleep. If you don't do something to help release the tension, your jaw can be painful and could become worse—in cases such as lockjaw, it's important to see your doctor or specialist. Your dentist can also help by giving you a mouth guard at night to stop you from grinding your teeth. This micro meditation will help release the tension in your jawline.

1 Using your thumb and forefinger, gently pinch your jawbone on each side of your face by your ear. If you feel more comfortable, you can use your middle finger too. While holding your fingers there, slowly open your mouth, hold for a couple of seconds, and close. Repeat this a few times.

2 Now slowly move your fingers along your jawline, applying a small amount of pressure as you move from your ear to your chin. Repeat this a few times.

3 Finally, massage your jaw by the side of your ears. With your three middle fingers flat against your face and your thumb gently supporting under your jawline, press into your cheeks. Hold your hands there for a few moments as though you're cupping your own face in your hands. Feel the warmth and comfort as you do this.

micro meditation
EAR RELEASE

Massaging your ears can give you a wonderful release if you're feeling anxious, stressed, or tense in any way. Physically it is great for helping to alleviate pain and mentally it releases endorphins, the feel-good chemical in your body. The amazing thing about massaging your ears is that you are touching acupressure points, known as the helix, in the outer fold of the ear, and in other places, too, which has a positive impact on relieving tension in the moment.

Another great and quick release for headaches or tension is to gently pinch and slowly pull down on your ear lobe. It works wonders—here's how to have a go.

1 Start by gently pressing the outer fold of your ear with your thumb and forefinger, from the top all the way down to your earlobe.

2 Gently press the lobe and start massaging it in circular movements with your thumb, forefinger, and middle finger.

3 Work your way up the outer part of your ear and back down again.

4 Repeat until you notice the wonderful release it can give you in moments. Remember to breathe!

micro meditation
IMAGINE A DANCING FLAME

A wonderful distraction when you want to feel some warmth and nurturing, this comforting micro meditation can help you if you've had a breakup (see page 44) or someone is blaming you for something that isn't your fault. It's also great at helping balance your emotions.

1 If you're at home or at work, find somewhere quiet and private to go like your bedroom or the restroom.

2 Close your eyes and take a slow, deep breath in through your nose and slowly out through your mouth. Now breathe normally.

3 Visualize flames dancing in your mind. Watch the different colors of orange, red, and golden yellow and the patterns they make. Feel the heat.

4 Notice how your thoughts have shifted.

micro meditation
ARM SOOTHER IN AN INSTANT

Touch can help relax you in different situations (see page 88). This micro meditation is not quite verging on being ticklish but gives a lovely, comforting feeling. Here's what to do:

1 Using the tips of your fingers and thumb, very lightly stroke up and down the inside of your forearm to your elbow several times.

2 Now use gentle, circular motions clockwise or counterclockwise around the inside of your elbow.

3 Switch to the other arm and repeat, or you may prefer to do this on one arm only— whatever feels more calming for you.

REAL LIFE STORY
LENNY SUE'S SOOTHING SOLUTION

Lenny Sue was feeling very anxious about being in the school pageant. She had been waiting for so long to be a cheerleader and it was her time to shine in front of her friends and family. Since she was a young child, her mum had always stroked her arm if she was worried or upset about anything. It became her go-to micro meditation every time she felt anxious. She did the Arm Soother in an Instant micro meditation (see opposite) whenever she felt upset, worried or anxious and it relaxed her mentally and physically in the moment.

micro meditation
HAND MASSAGE

There are times you just need to give yourself a moment to breathe and find your inner calm. This hand cream massage meditation is always a favorite with my students and clients. I use my wonderful, rose-fragranced hand cream and apply some to each of their hands. It's comforting and soothing in the moment, and you can do it anytime and anywhere. Please note if you don't have any hand cream available, you can still give your hands a lovely massage as a wonderful distraction if you need a moment or two for yourself to just be and relax.

1 Choose a hand cream with a fragrance you love, which absorbs easily. There are so many you can choose from. I'm a huge fan of rose-scented hand cream, which makes me feel totally calm and relaxed. Maybe you love orange blossom, strawberry, or lavender scents. Whatever it is, choose a scent that makes you feel good in the moment and gives your hands a delicious fragrance.

2 Keep a tube or pot on your desk at work, on the countertop in your kitchen, in the TV room, by your bed, in your bag, or anywhere you can reach it easily when you need it in the moment!

3 Squeeze some of the cream into the palm of one of your hands and start massaging it in slowly. Massage into the back of your hand, then slowly massage each finger and fingertip at a time.

4 Spend a minute massaging each hand. Stay focused on what you are doing. Feel how soothing and calming it is and notice how much more relaxed you feel. If you start thinking about the shopping or a friend or client you haven't called back, STOP the mind chatter and come back to focusing on massaging your hands.

5 Take a slow, deep breath in through your nose and then slowly out through your mouth.

6 Repeat this process several times a day when you need to and enjoy the fragrant smell of your hand cream to remind you of your moments of calm.

REAL LIFE STORY
AVA'S MOMENT OF CALM

Ava was having a challenging day at work. It was one of those days when whatever she did wasn't right. It was clear her boss was not in a good mood, and she realized he was taking it out on her! She was so upset.

Ava remembered the lovely hand massage I showed her how to do in my workshop. She took out her favorite hand cream from her desk drawer and focused on giving herself a brief, mini hand massage. As she slowly massaged her palms, the back of her hands, and each finger, she felt as if it completely transported her to a place of total calm. It took her less than two minutes to feel better, the massage completely distracted her from feeling upset or angry, and she felt calm and relaxed. She took a deep breath and finished the list her boss was chasing her for. Other micro meditations that will work in these situations include Ear Release (see page 108) and Stop and Touch (see page 89).

"Calm your mind and open your heart to new possibilities which will help you to feel happy, peaceful, and in control once again."

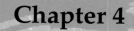

Chapter 4

Crystal Magic
and Chakras for
Micro Meditation

The Magic of Crystals 116

Working with the Chakras 136

The Magic of Crystals

I was born by the sea and from a young age was always fascinated by the shells I found on the sand. I loved collecting them. One day, I was given a rose quartz crystal by my Grandma Kay. It was pink, shiny, and magical and it made me feel special and loved. In my teenage years I discovered more and more about crystals and, as an adult, I have spent many years experiencing the power of these incredible stones.

I am a great believer in traditional and holistic medicine as it has so much to offer. Alongside traditional medicines, crystals can give you what you need for comfort, healing, confidence, and so much more through their amazing energy and vibrations. I have worked with them myself, and to help others, with everything from positive thinking to managing stress, anxiety, and overwhelm, which is why I felt it important to include crystals and chakras in this book and give them their own special chapter.

All crystals can help you with many things, and over the following pages I suggest 20 crystals that can help you in different situations. Simply keep them with you by the side of your bed, under your pillow, in your bag, pocket, bra, on the countertop in the kitchen, or anywhere in your home where you can reach them in the moment. Remember to keep them out of the reach of children or pets! I have focused on some main areas you may need help with, so you can choose different crystals for any situation, or when you need a particular crystal for your micro meditations, from managing anger or grief to energy boosters. Work with crystals alongside any of the micro meditations in this book by holding them while meditating—if you are about to shout at your partner or kids, are feeling conflict at work or in your relationships at home, feeling frustrated or overwhelmed, they can put you in a calmer, more relaxed state of mind!

If you haven't yet experienced the power of crystals, be open to all that is new. Enjoy the extra sparkle and light that crystals bring to your life. They may just give you positive shifts you never imagined possible.

THE MALACHITE MEDITATION FOR SLEEP

Lack of sleep can be exhausting and emotionally draining (see page 24).
The crystal malachite is unique and special as it can help give you a peaceful
night's sleep when your mind is racing and full of a million things you just can't seem
to shift. Take your crystal to bed and hold it for a couple of minutes to feel the
benefits. Continue holding it while you sleep or place it under your pillow or by the
side of your bed. This can also help you if you're feeling depressed and need a boost.

THE GARNET TWO-MINUTE POWER NAP
TO BOOST YOUR ENERGY

There may be times during your day when you need a quick power nap
to feel refreshed and revitalized. Garnet is the perfect crystal to give
you the energy boost you need.

Find somewhere quiet to sit or lie down. Set an alarm for two
minutes and hold your garnet crystal in your hand. Close your eyes
and, as you focus on the crystal, feel a surge of energy flow through
you. Notice how much more get-up-and-go you have after only two
minutes have passed!

POSITIVE CRYSTAL BOOSTERS FOR A NEGATIVE MINDSET

Quartz is an amazing crystal that can be found in most of the technology that we plug into electrical circuits, like washing machines, phones, televisions, computers, spaceships, cars, and so much more. You can feel the positive vibrations from this crystal just by being near some of these machines, but if sitting in front of your washing machine isn't your thing (it's certainly not everyone's!), I suggest holding your quartz crystal at different times during the day at home or work to give you the boost you need. You'll notice a shift in energy—and maybe tingling or warmth in your hand—in the first 30 seconds.

Other crystals that can help you with negative thoughts or the negativity of others (see pages 62–63) are tourmaline, obsidian, and pyrite.

REAL LIFE STORY
QUARTZ VIBRATIONS

Quartz crystals can be literally everywhere technology allows and when teaching a crystal healing course, I shared this exciting information with the class. One of my students took this literally. She was feeling negative about everything going on in her life and needed a positive shift, so she sat in front of her washing machine for the final couple of minutes of the spin cycle. She said watching the machine going round and round, listening to the white noise, and repeating positive affirmations that we had talked about made her feel great. The quartz vibrations certainly gave her the boost she needed to start feeling more positive. Today, if she's putting a few loads of laundry on during the day, she pops back to the machine for a quick refresher and feels totally revitalized!

PAIN MANAGEMENT WITH QUARTZ

Quartz is also the go-to crystal for many healers. One of its many healing qualities is that it can help manage pain in moments. For example, if you have neck ache, backache, shoulder ache, or any other aches, or if your child falls over and cuts or grazes their knee or elbow, or has a tummy ache, it really helps ease the pain.

There are lots of micro meditations throughout this book for coping with pain, both mentally and physically (see page 42), and you can work with your quartz crystal in combination with any of these meditations. For bumps and bruises, you can also try the Quick Pain Relief with Quartz micro meditation on the next page.

micro meditation
QUICK PAIN RELIEF WITH QUARTZ

This crystal micro meditation will help you to manage pain in the moment. If you or a loved one, friend, or colleague have hurt themselves badly, always get the problem checked out by a professional.

1 Hold your quartz crystal with the point, known as a termination, above the area where you are feeling pain.

2 Circle the termination in a clockwise motion, 1–2in (2.5–5cm) above the area. You may feel a vibration, a pulling in your hand, or a cool, warm, or tingly sensation in the area you are holding the crystal over.

3 Continue for 1–2 minutes more.

4 Notice how much better the pain is—maybe it's even gone away completely!

FEEL CALM AND STOP WORRYING WITH GREEN CALCITE

Green calcite is a totally fabulous crystal to calm and relax you. If you're having a stressful day and everything is overwhelming, there are so many different situations that green calcite can help you with. For example, see Mike's story, Taking Control of Anxiety (page 16). Other stressful situations might include:

- You're stuck in traffic and late for an appointment.

- The meeting you've planned for months has been cancelled at the last minute.

- Maybe you're anxious about an interview.

- You're about to go on a first date.

- Every time you go to the dentist.

I keep a piece of green calcite in my car, in my bag, and on my side table, or under my pillow at night. You can even keep a piece in your bra or pocket. I also find it helpful to keep green calcite by my computer and in the therapy room next to me when I'm seeing clients or giving treatments. It works wonders and is perfect for a de-stressing crystal micro meditation. The moment you feel anxious, worried, or stressed about anything, hold your green calcite. Take a slow, deep breath in through your nose and slow breath out through your mouth. You'll notice a difference in an instant—and you may feel warmth or tingling in your hand too!

FOCUS WITH RAINBOW FLUORITE

Rainbow fluorite gives you instant focus. Hold it at different times throughout your day or whenever you need to feel the energy and vibrations of this powerful stone— you'll feel a surge of energy that enables you to be in the moment. This very quick and powerful micro meditation can help if you're finding it a challenge to feel motivated at work or home, or if you're having difficulties talking to friends, family, and colleagues. You'll notice in moments that you feel inspired to write the report you were unable to focus on, or instantly focus as you find yourself back in the room once more joining in the conversation.

Rainbow fluorite is also an amazing deterrent if there's someone manipulative in your life. Keep it nearby or in your purse or pocket and hold it when this person is around. A client of mine had a very manipulative ex-boyfriend and wanted to keep him away. She kept a piece of rainbow fluorite with her cell phone, by her computer, and in her purse. Whenever he tried to contact her, she held the crystal and he went away without bothering her!

Fluorite is also a wonderful crystal to protect you from electromagnetic fog. Keep a piece by your computer, phone, television, and any other technical products to keep the electromagnetic rays at bay.

ANGER MANAGEMENT WITH SNOWFLAKE OBSIDIAN

It's natural to feel angry when someone says or does something to annoy you. How you manage this in the moment can have a huge impact on your own well-being. Shouting and screaming out loud can be a great release for you (see page 23). So, too, can exercise, such as putting on the boxing gloves and getting in the ring or hitting the bag. This isn't always practical in some situations though! For example:

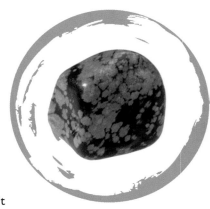

• Experiencing road rage.

• Being angry at a colleague because they let you down and didn't do what they said they would.

• Friends who keep cancelling on you and making your friendship seem unimportant.

• A family member who comments negatively on everything you're doing and never mentions anything positive.

When a situation or person infuriates you and you want to lash out, STOP! Hold the crystal snowflake obsidian, then take a deep breath slowly in through your nose and slowly out through your mouth. Repeat twice more. This helps control your emotions, especially when you feel ready to explode, go red in the face, or say the wrong thing to someone! Staying calm and looking at things rationally is a much better solution for your health and well-being.

GET CREATIVE WITH CARNELIAN

Have you lost your creative spark? Are you are looking for motivation and inspiration? Well, carnelian is the perfect crystal to give you the creative boost you need.

Keep carnelian with you wherever you go. If you're sitting staring at a blank page on your computer, stop and practice this very effective micro meditation. Hold your crystal for a couple of minutes throughout the day. You'll feel a surge of inspiration flow through you and notice that your creative spark suddenly comes back.

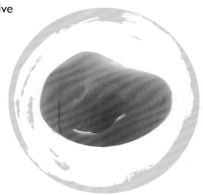

SNOW QUARTZ TO CLEAR YOUR MIND

If you're having a worry wobble (see page 20) or worrisome thoughts of any kind, snow quartz helps take these thoughts out of your mind. It clears your headspace, which gives you the opportunity to think about new, positive things. Snow quartz will stop any negative chatter and enable you to feel clearer in your mind if you have something important you need to do, such as:

• Take a driving test.

• Decide whether to move away from home.

• Accept an amazing job opportunity.

• Sign the final completion papers to buy or rent a new home.

This is also a great crystal for children and teenagers to help them stop worrying before their exams. There is a lovely aura around this milky-white crystal that is emotionally comforting too.

BE COURAGEOUS WITH TIGER'S EYE

Whenever I see the crystal tiger's eye, it always reminds me of the cowardly lion character in the movie *The Wizard of Oz*. During the movie, his confidence came shining through eventually, but I wish he'd had a tiger's eye crystal to hold and believe in himself! This crystal, with its beautiful markings and incredible vibrations and energy, can help if you're feeling afraid or worried, especially if there is something you really want to do but these feelings keep stopping you or are holding you back. For example:

• Take an amazing vacation, but you don't feel confident to fly.

• Walk into a roomful of people you don't know on your own.

• Go on a first date (see page 66).

Next time you feel afraid, hold a tiger's eye crystal. As you hold it, tell yourself "I can do this," "I believe in myself," or "I feel confident" (see also Positive Affirmations, pages 64–65). The energy from this crystal will give you the courage and confidence you need.

REAL LIFE STORY
EMILY'S MOMENT OF COURAGE

Emily was introduced to Antoine by her friend Clara. Emily liked
Antoine, but she was feeling very nervous and pessimistic about going
on their first date. Emily called me to ask what she should do, as
all her other dates had been disasters! I suggested she hold her
tiger's eye crystal and keep it with her during the evening. The
moment Emily met Antoine, the chemistry between them was
amazing. They didn't stop talking and laughing the whole evening. It
was a huge relief for her that he was a really nice person, and they got
on well. They have been dating ever since!

FEEL CONFIDENT WITH CRAZY LACE AGATE

Crazy lace agate and tiger's eye are wonderful crystals that complement each other
and give you an extra boost of confidence and courage. Try carrying them with you.
The fabulous crazy lace agate crystal is especially helpful when your self-esteem is low.
It will give you the self-belief to have a more positive attitude and feel better about
yourself and your abilities, so that you can achieve the things you want to. For example:

- Perhaps you don't feel good enough to go for the job you want or to set up your
  own business.

- You would like to speak out about a situation that you've been blamed
  for when it's not your fault.

- Maybe someone is not taking no for an answer, and you need
  to be firm but nice without upsetting them.

- Sometimes you feel your friends decide what they want to
  do without letting you get a word in to say what you want.

To manage these kinds of situations, you can practice Positive Affirmations (see pages 64–65) or try anchoring (see page 40). Another wonderful micro meditation is to always keep your crazy lace agate crystal with you—invest in a crystal bracelet or pendant, so you can wear it all the time. Have a stone to hold, too. Keep the stone in your bag, pocket, or somewhere easy to reach, so you can hold it throughout your day for a couple of minutes whenever you need a confidence boost.

When you start to believe in yourself, your confidence will come shining through. You'll notice how you can suddenly say what you want because you believe in yourself again and know you can do anything.

GIVE YOURSELF LOVE AND NURTURING WITH ROSE QUARTZ

Rose quartz is the crystal of love for yourself and others. It gives off the love vibe just by looking at it! When you're not giving yourself enough love, this is the perfect crystal to provide you the nurturing you need. Maybe you could wear a heart rose quartz pendant or crystal bracelet. Having rose quartz in your home or at work introduces a special sense of beauty and peace. It's gentle and yet so powerful and giving.

Meditating with this beautiful crystal is very soothing. I always give my students and clients a rose quartz to hold during a class or one-to-one session, so they are able to focus on themselves and the love they deserve.

REAL LIFE STORY
TIME FOR YOU: DOLLY'S WAY

Dolly has three children aged four to seven. She works three days a week as a physical education teacher at a junior high school (middle school). On her days off she shops, cooks, cleans, and does everything she can to give her family a lovely home. Dolly makes sure she's there for her children at every school event, helps them with their homework, and loves giving them all she can. Dolly was constantly on the go and wasn't giving herself the love and self-care she needed. If she wasn't doing the laundry, she was catching up on phone calls or text messages. She gave herself no "me time." Dolly realized she needed help, but her husband travels regularly for his work and her family live too far away.

When she came to see me for a session, the first thing I did was put a rose quartz crystal in each of her hands. She felt a warm, tingly feeling in her hands and immediately relaxed. I asked her to close her eyes, take a slow, deep breath in through her nose and slowly out through her mouth, and remember a time she did something for herself that made her feel good, such as a soothing massage. We also explored different micro meditations that would work for Dolly, including anchoring (see page 40), going for a walk in nature (see page 83), and enjoying a soothing drink (see page 85). Dolly loved the idea of making herself a hot chocolate drink with marshmallows on the top as she was always doing this for her children but never herself!

These micro meditations became part of her daily routine. She even treated herself to a rose quartz heart pendant and kept a rose quartz crystal in her purse, the car, by her bed, and, most importantly, one to hold every evening when she relaxed with a movie and her delicious hot chocolate drink. If her husband was home, he was delighted to see Dolly was finally giving herself the love and attention she needed to take care of herself too.

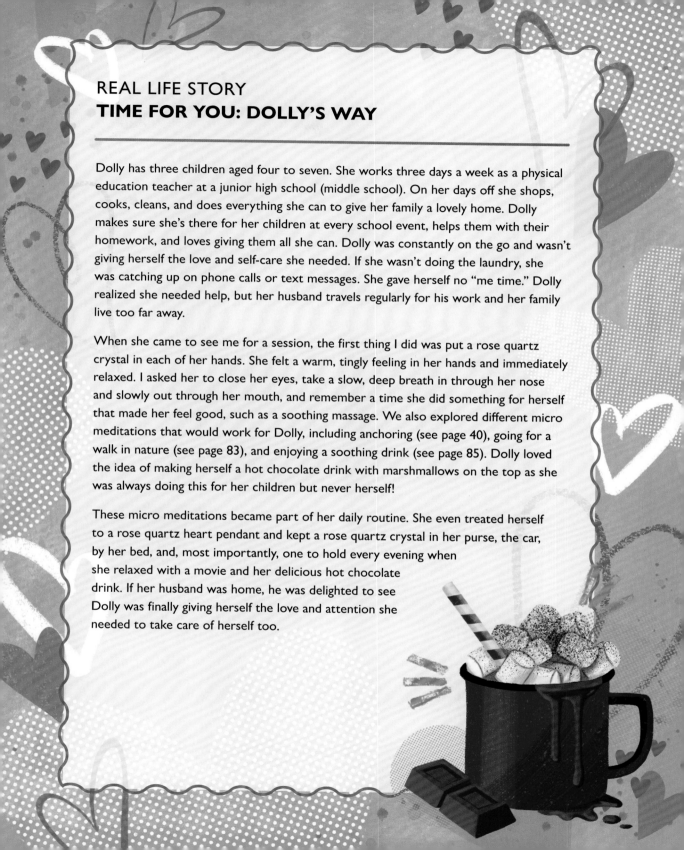

CONTROL YOUR ANXIETY AND RELEASE HEADACHES WITH AMETHYST

Just looking at the beautiful purple color of an amethyst crystal is soothing and healing. Different types of amethyst will help you with mild to chronic headaches.

- Pale amethyst: Good for mild recurring headaches.

- Dark amethyst: Will help you with intense headaches and migraines.

- Chevron amethyst: Helps with chronic migraines.

As a chronic pain sufferer with three plates and six screws in my head—and my infamous loose screw!—I will often hold a chevron amethyst. Holding this crystal while doing my positive affirmation micro meditation (see page 43) is very powerful and effective. The one I say frequently from the moment I wake up every morning is "I'm in control of you, you're not in control of me," which is directed at the pain. Migraine sufferers will find this technique particularly soothing as their head pain starts to release. If you have a mild headache or a more intense one coming on, I suggest holding your amethyst crystal, drinking lots of water to hydrate, and then focusing on your breathing. Feel the crystal in your hand and notice how this helps you.

All of these different and amazing amethyst crystals give a very powerful healing vibration and energy. While they will help with different levels of headaches, they are also good for anxiety. Holding one of these magical crystals will enable you to manage any emotions that you are feeling. There are different micro meditations for anxiety which you can do while holding your amethyst crystal, including Release Your Anxiety (see page 18) and Count and Breathe in Stressful Moments (see page 49).

LET GO OF UPSET WITH PINK TOURMALINE

If you've experienced a relationship breakup, lost your job, or have had an upset with a friend or family member (see page 44), pink tourmaline has a very gentle way of helping you heal your emotions and gives you the comfort and love you need. If you're upset about a person or situation, hold pink tourmaline. Notice how much calmer, more relaxed, and better about yourself you feel after a minute or two. It is also the perfect crystal to help you build new relationships, feel motivated, and protect you from unwanted negative energy.

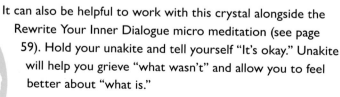

RELEASE RELATIONSHIP SADNESS WITH UNAKITE

When a relationship doesn't work out it can be so upsetting. You may question why and what you did wrong. Or perhaps you may be grieving the loss of a friend or family member. If you didn't get on, or you didn't receive the love you wanted from the relationship, maybe you find it hard to understand why you are so sad. When things don't work out the way you want them to, we often grieve for the loss of what we didn't have.

The unakite crystal helps you with these emotions. When you're feeling upset because you wish things had been better with you and your friend, or your father or mother, for example, hold this crystal for a couple of minutes at different times during your day and evening. Focus on the good memories and what and who is in your life now.

It can also be helpful to work with this crystal alongside the Rewrite Your Inner Dialogue micro meditation (see page 59). Hold your unakite and tell yourself "It's okay." Unakite will help you grieve "what wasn't" and allow you to feel better about "what is."

MANAGE YOUR GRIEF
WITH SMOKY QUARTZ

Grief takes you on a rollercoaster journey with waves
of different emotions that can affect you at any time. Dr.
Elisabeth Kübler-Ross describes the five stages of grief as
denial, anger, bargaining, depression, and acceptance, although
you may not necessarily experience them in this order. Smoky
quartz has an amazing, healing energy that will help you to manage
these emotions—and many more—as you work through them.

Losing my father was devastating and felt surreal, as
though the sadness took over my whole being. I kept
smoky quartz with me wherever I went. If I felt a wave
of emotion come over me, I held the quartz tightly
and it gave me comfort, unconditional love, support,
and understanding. I also found many of the micro
meditations in this book very comforting and you
might find they help you, too. Try A Walk in the Woods
or Park (see page 83) or Tapping into Your Senses (see
pages 88–97) while you hold your smoky quartz.

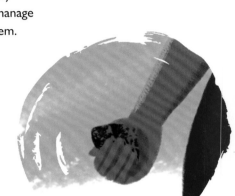

SAY WHAT YOU FEEL WITH KYANITE

It can be frustrating when you are bursting to say something, and you think you can't:

• Have you ever wanted to say what you feel and the words wouldn't come out?

• Do you sometimes feel intimidated by the people you are talking to?

• In meetings, does no one let you get a word in edgeways as they think they know best?

Kyanite is the best crystal to help you get those words out and is my number
one choice for communication. Holding kyanite when you want to say
something will help you say what you want with clarity and confidence.
It is absolutely the crystal to keep with you in any scenario where
you need the extra help to speak out and say what you wish.
You can also work with kyanite alongside micro meditations
such as Anchor Away Your Frustrations (see page 40) and
Manifest in a Moment (see page 70).

REAL LIFE STORY
DANNY'S PRESENTATION

Danny had recently passed his nutritional therapy degree and was so happy to get a job consulting for a popular supplement brand. He was told he would be working with professors and other senior medical professionals, which was quite overwhelming. Danny was asked to make a presentation to his fellow nutritionists. However, he felt that he was lost for words. He was worried about how he would come across and whether he would say the right thing.

During our video one-to-one session, Danny and I talked about his knowledge of the subject, his abilities, and his achievements. I reminded him that, although he was talking to fellow nutritionists, they didn't know everything he was going to say—if he missed a sentence or two, they would be none the wiser! I also suggested he use prompt cards with key words to refer to if he needed a quick reminder. Sometimes nervous energy or an adrenaline rush can be a good thing and help you do even better. Having the trust and belief in your own abilities and knowledge will also reassure you.

I also suggested Danny hold kyanite during his presentation, which would inspire him to speak and feel confident in doing. Danny had two of these amazing crystals. He wore one as a pendant and kept another in his pocket to hold for a couple of minutes before he started to speak. His first talk went brilliantly; everyone was very impressed with his confidence and how well he came across.

ORGANIZE YOUR MIND WITH LAPIS LAZULI

Are your drawers and cabinets at home and work organized? Or do you let everything get messy and every so often have a massive tidy-up? Just like your surroundings, if you have too many chatterboxes in your head and need to organize your mind, you may feel you are unable to get anything done (see Boxing Your Thoughts, page 27). The crystal lapis lazuli is an amazing organizer! It can help you to plan and get things in order. This crystal will help you if you have:

- A party to arrange.

- Several emails to write.

- An evening out with friends to organize.

Just one or two minutes holding this powerful crystal several times a day will tidy up your busy mind and help you get things done.

FEEL AN INSTANT POSITIVE SHIFT

Citrine is wonderful for change and is the perfect stone for new beginnings. Sometimes life's frustrations can get you down and you need a magical light to shine down on you and say: "Hey, everything's going to work out" (see Annie's Positive Shift, page 53). Hold the stone, focus on it, and let its natural vibrations and energy help you to feel good and bring sunshine and success into your life.

Citrine is also known as the money stone and is a fabulous crystal to keep in your purse or your pocket, on your desk or nightstand, or under your pillow at night. Wherever you keep it, be sure to embrace this beautiful, golden crystal throughout your day. It can give you the newfound freedom of exciting things to come and is the perfect crystal for abundance in every way.

Orange calcite can also make you smile and feel good, and give you a happy boost. This happy and calming crystal will certainly get you laughing, smiling, and feeling so much better in the moment. Hold it for one or two minutes and notice how you just can't resist smiling!

GROUND YOURSELF WITH HEMATITE

Hematite will help you rebalance your mind and body and reconnect with the earth. There may be times you feel light-headed or upset in certain situations. While there are lots of micro meditations that can help with overwhelm (see pages 22–31), simply holding your hematite stone can also be a wonderful, grounding experience in the moment.

micro meditation
HEMATITE FOR GROUNDING

If you have two hematite crystals, this micro meditation is great for restoring balance when you want to feel grounded in the moment because everything is too much and you are feeling woozy or light-headed.

1 If you have immediate access to the outside at work or at home, or you are in a park, take your shoes and socks off and stand in the grass as you feel the earth beneath your feet.

2 Hold one hematite crystal in each hand.

3 Breathe as you feel your feet become more solid and stable on the ground. Imagine you have roots growing from the base of your feet deep into the earth.

4 Notice how much more balanced, grounded, and stable you feel.

Working with the Chakras

Your chakras are wonderful wheels of energy that give you the power to embrace life and feel open to many possibilities. We focus on seven main chakras that run down the center of your body from your head to the base of your spine. If they become blocked, you may feel stuck in certain situations such as creativity, confidence, or love. Once they open up, you will notice how certain areas begin to flow. When practicing your micro meditations, you may find it helpful to focus on the relevant chakra, so you can open up to the endless possibilities and flow you need to move forward in your life. Each chakra is shown with a crystal in the traditional rainbow colors associated with each chakra; all of the chakra micro meditations can be enhanced by including the relevant crystal.

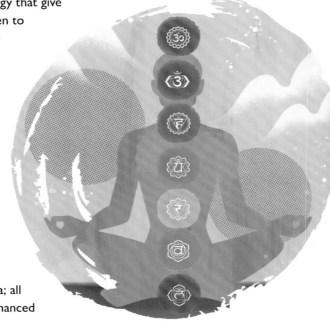

CROWN CHAKRA (SAHASRARA)

This is the beautiful chakra that oversees all your chakras! It is over your crown above your head and gives you inspiration while also increasing your awareness of everything around you. By focusing on opening this chakra you are embracing everything your feel, see, hear, and touch. It lifts your mood and connects you spiritually so you feel more intuitive, inspired, and creative. Amethyst is associated with the Crown chakra.

MICRO MEDITATION Take a slow, deep breath in through your nose and imagine seeing or feeling a wonderful purple light around the crown of your head and going up to the sky. As you breathe out, see or feel this light surrounding your body like a purple shower of inspiration!

THIRD EYE (AJNA)

Your Third Eye chakra is just above your eyebrows in the center of your forehead. Opening up this chakra can help us be so much more productive. When your Third Eye chakra, also known as the Brow chakra, is open and awakened, even mundane tasks such as tidying your closet or your children's rooms can seem so much more straightforward. When planning and organizing a social function such as a party, sporting event, or charity night, if you notice you feel stuck and nothing is flowing, then it can help you get your focus back. Lapis lazuli is associated with the Third Eye chakra.

MICRO MEDITATION Place your hands on your forehead over your Third Eye. Imagine seeing or feeling a deep blue light shining out in front of you. You may feel the vibrations and energy shooting from your Third Eye as you begin to feel so much more focused.

THROAT CHAKRA (VISHUDDHA)

Your Throat chakra can be found at the base of the throat. It is there to help you speak your truth and say what you want to without holding back—within reason! Speaking out is something you may feel embarrassed or shy to do. For example, are you nervous or anxious about giving a talk to a roomful of people? Or perhaps you are worried about telling a friend they have hurt you and you want to resolve the situation? Opening up your Throat chakra will help you to say what you feel with clarity and confidence. Blue lace agate is associated with the Throat chakra.

MICRO MEDITATION Place your hands, one over the other, at the base of your throat. Imagine a light blue light shining brightly from your throat. Feel it tingle and stimulate your vocal cords as you feel ready to speak out.

HEART CHAKRA (ANAHATA)

The Heart chakra is located in the center of the chest. When your Heart chakra is open, flowing, and well-balanced, it is full of love, compassion, and forgiveness. When it's blocked it can hold so much anger, jealousy, grief, and hatred. Giving yourself love is a huge part of your well-being. During unsettling times—such as a broken relationship, loss of a loved one, or job redundancy or retirement—opening your Heart chakra to allow healing to begin can give you a wonderful sense of peace and happiness. Malachite is associated with the Heart chakra.

MICRO MEDITATION Place your hand on your heart. Imagine sending yourself love, compassion, and empathy. Keep practicing this for 30–60 seconds throughout your day. Notice the feeling of peace and tranquility within you.

SOLAR PLEXUS (MANIPURA)

You can find the Solar Plexus chakra just under your breastbone in the center of your body. Low self-esteem and confidence can prevent you from doing so many things. Your Solar Plexus chakra can help lift your mood and give you a boost of confidence to do anything you want—for example, walk into a room of people you don't know (see page 66), stand up to give a presentation (see page 133), get dressed up and go out on a date (see pages 66–67), or even join a fun dance class you've wanted to do for a long time but felt too self-conscious. Citrine is associated with the Solar Plexus chakra.

MICRO MEDITATION Place your hands on your solar plexus. Imagine seeing a golden glow from the area. You might feel vibrations or warmth, too. Notice your self-confidence start to flow as you feel so much better about yourself. Start making plans to do the things you have always wanted to do.

SACRAL CHAKRA (SVADHISTHANA)

Your Sacral chakra is just below your belly button. Focus on this chakra any time you feel the need to see your creative ideas flow! For example, perhaps your creative side isn't flowing at work, you're unable to come up with fun ideas for your little one's birthday party, or you need to find a fabulous outfit for your friend's birthday party or a rock concert. Carnelian is associated with the Sacral chakra.

MICRO MEDITATION Place your hands on your Sacral chakra. Imagine or see an orange color burning brightly or feel its warmth in the area. As you keep repeating this mini meditation, notice the amazing creative ideas coming into your head.

BASE CHAKRA (MULADHARA)

Your Base chakra, otherwise known as your Root chakra, is at the base of your spine. To find it, place your hand there and then bring it round to the front of your pelvic area. When you're feeling lightheaded or overwhelmed your Base chakra will help you to feel more grounded, balanced, secure, and steady, with your feet firmly on the ground. Red jasper is associated with the Base chakra.

MICRO MEDITATION If you're outside, you could go barefoot on the grass or feel the mud beneath your feet. Focus on your Base chakra. Place your hands on the base of your spine, or over your pelvic area if that feels more comfortable. Imagine a deep red color flowing from your Base chakra. See it traveling down your legs to your feet. Imagine you have roots coming out the base of your feet that grow deep into the ground. Remember to breathe! As you begin to feel more grounded and calmer, any feeling of lightheadedness or overwhelm will disappear.

Moments to Remember

It has been so fabulous and special writing this book for you from beginning to end. It includes many different situations, case studies, and micro meditations that I hope have given you alternatives to choose from when times are challenging and you need to reach out for help.

These pages are full of stories and fabulous illustrations that may resonate with you and are there to remind and encourage you to make the changes you need in moments and not wait for things to get worse. If you need some self-nurturing, have you given yourself a wonderful arm and/or face soother to indulge yourself with? Or have you started to practice taking those slow, deep breaths to calm you or splashing your face with cold water? Maybe reaching out for a tub of ice cream or placing your hands on a tree to feel some positive energy is something you have loved doing or are about to step outside and do! Perhaps you have started singing at the sink with your own washing-up brush as your microphone or are enjoying the different seasonal micro meditations? Family mealtimes can also become quite fraught on occasion and mindful eating may be the ideal solution for you too!

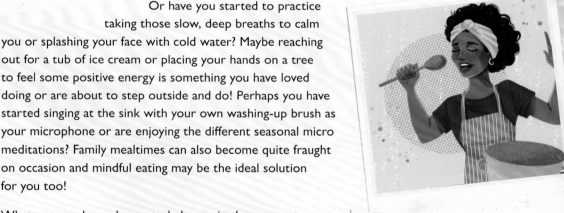

Whatever you have chosen to help you in the moment I wish you much love and peace in your heart. I also wish you beautiful energy so you can be happy and healthy, and have some fun in your life irrespective of what else is going on around you. Step out of your situation and into your micro meditation and enjoy every moment!

Big hugs,

Micro Meditation Poem

If you're anxious or stressed and emotions are high,
These micro meditations will help you get by.
For positive focus in seconds not days
Help is at hand to give you so many ways.

Micro meditations give you tools to make change.
There are anchors and laughter going through every stage,
From counting and breathing to splashing your face.
It's amazing how quickly you're back in your headspace.
These magical moments give you peace and calm.
You can micro meditate just by stroking your arm!

There's hot chocolate and marshmallows and all things nice.
This special indulgence gives you a fabulous spice.
Mindful eating gives you time to breathe
When others are frustrating, and you need to leave!

It's amazing how your senses give you so much.
There are wonderful moments just to focus on touch!
From Sight and Sound to Taste and Smell,
Here are many micro meditations you can do to feel well.

If you're frustrated, angry, or feeling let down,
The shifts you'll have will turn everything around.
Counting backward from ten is a great distraction.
Your worry wobbles now have a call to action.

Nature takes you to a place of calm.
The trees and the flowers are full of charm.
Your health and well-being are number one.
Remember to take care and have some fun.

There are crystals and chakras waiting to share
And a micro meditation that tells you to focus and stare!
Your imagination can help you release
Any overwhelm you're feeling to give you some peace.

With visualization and stepping into the new,
It's time to micro meditate and bring back the positive you.

Index

PICTURE CREDITS

t = top; b = bottom; l = left; r = right; c = center
All illustrations by Camila Gray © CICO Books except the following: © Adobe Stock / Eva Speshneva (frame): pages 2, 76, 79, 81, 84; Elena Pimukova (frame): page 86; Arthit: pages 16, 106; warmworld: pages 20, 59, 60b; StudioGraphic (boxes): page 27; Olga: pages 33, 119b; standby: page 37; gomolach: page 38; WinWin: pages 52, 55r, 64, 65; Tartila: page 68t; Pixel Pine: pages 76t, 76br; Sumondesigner_42: page 76bl, 76tr; Maria: page 103; MicroOne: page 119t; Ekaterina: page 131t. Crystal photography © CICO Books by Roy Palmer and Geoff Dann, pages 117, 118, 121, 122, 124, 125, 126, 127, 128, 130, 131b, 132, 134, 135, 136, 137t, 137b, 138, 139.

Acknowledgments

Thank you for being you, my readers!

To my amazing students and clients, you are a constant inspiration. Seeing the positive changes in you as you continue your journey makes me so happy and motivates me to do even more.

Words cannot express how grateful I am to my fabulous friend Philip Permutt. Thank you for your constant support and inspiration. And to our most gorgeous dogs Teddy and Honey who I adore so much. Your unconditional doggie love is very special. Even when writing until the early hours you are constantly there on my lap or beside me!

To my wonderful family and friends. You are constantly there supporting and believing in me, especially my amazing mother Valerie, my son and daughter Adam and Gemma, my daughter-in-law Emma, son-in-law Adam, niece Katie Kit Kat, nephew Jason, and my sister and brother-in-law Boo and Keith. ♥ ♥

Zoe Jacobson, James Demetris, Xenia Capsalis, Yen Doan, and Anna Le, your continued support throughout the year means so much. The hair and beauty world wouldn't be the same without you!

Jason Raineri, personal trainer extraordinaire and PA regularly when I had so many ideas that needed writing down immediately for this book while I was lifting weights or on the rowing machine! Thank you for your patience and encouragement! Daniel Daggett, you are the best sports massage therapist and listener!

Jennifer Vanderwerf, Ashley Harris, and Emma Parker, thank you so much for your ongoing media support.

To everyone at CICO Books who has made this book come to life, especially Carmel Edmonds who helped make this book possible and Kristy Richardson for your care and positive energy. Thank you to all in the design department, especially Sally Powell and Emily Breen, and to Camila Gray for your beautiful illustrations.

Claire and Becky, I really appreciate your constant help setting up workshops and courses for me and helping with everything while I have written this book and so much more throughout the year.

When writing this book I spent many weeks at my favorite well-being retreat and happy place Shanti-Som in the Andalucian countryside in Spain. The peace, calm, and inspiration I feel while there is magical. It's so special having wonderful treatments, doing pilates and yoga, and teaching your guests relaxing meditations in such a stunning setting. Thank you to the brilliant manager Alicia and all your dedicated and caring team.

My beautiful grandsons Louis, Charlie, Toby, and Jack, you always make me smile and bring the brightest sunshine into my heart. Your fun and laughter fill me with so much happiness.

I feel very blessed and so grateful to have you all in my life. Thank you.

Love you all,

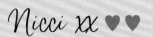 

Nicci xx ♥ ♥